Advance Praise for *The Political Economy of Agrarian Extractivism*

Academics and activists who are interested in the politics of agrarian, food, environmental, and political democratization issues must read McKay's compelling book: an empirically rich and theoretically brilliant book on agrarian extractivism.

— Saturnino M. Borras Jr., professor of Agrarian Studies, International Institute of Social Studies; editor-in-chief of the *Journal of Peasant Studies* and co-author of *The Politics of Transnational Agrarian Movements.*

Ben M. McKay provides an advanced analysis of the ways in which large-scale destructive agriculture operates, using its power to nullify various forms of resistance, while revealing how even those promising projects like Evo Morales' "Agrarian Revolution" in Bolivia can end up promoting an (agro)extractivist model. This book is vital for anyone interested in deepening their analysis of contemporary agrarian issues and politics.

— Gonzalo Colque, executive director, Fundación TIERRA, Bolivia

McKay's powerful analysis challenges dominant discourses to reveal the highly extractive nature of the industrial soy complex in Bolivia. With rich empirical detail, he shows how the underlying dynamics of agrarian extractivism generate social exclusion and environmental harm.

— Jennifer Clapp, Canada Research Chair in Global Food Security and Sustainability and professor in the School of Environment, Resources and Sustainability at the University of Waterloo, Canada

The Political Economy of Agrarian Extractivism: Lessons from Bolivia

ALSO IN THE CRITICAL DEVELOPMENT STUDIES SERIES

Development in Latin America: Toward a New Future (2019)
by Maristella Svampa, translation by Mark Rushton

Politics Rules: Power, Globalization and Development (2019)
by Adam Sneyd

Critical Development Studies: An Introduction (2018)
by Henry Veltmeyer & Raúl Delgado Wise

The Political Economy of Agrarian Extractivism: Lessons from Bolivia

BEN M. MCKAY

CRITICAL DEVELOPMENT STUDIES

FERNWOOD PUBLISHING

Practical ACTION PUBLISHING

Practical Action Publishing Ltd
27a Albert Street, Rugby, Warwickshire, CV21 2SG, UK
www.practicalactionpublishing.org

Published in North America by Fernwood Publishing, Canada, 2020
This edition published by Practical Action Publishing Ltd, 2020

A catalogue record for this book is available from the British Library.
A catalogue record for this book has been requested from the Library of Congress.

ISBN 978-1-78853-137-5 Paperback
ISBN 978-1-78853-138-2 Hardback
ISBN 978-1-78853-139-9 Ebook
ISBN 978-1-78853-140-5 Library PDF

Citation: McKay, B.M.(2020) *The Political Economy of Agrarian Extractivism: lessons from Bolivia*, Rugby, UK: Practical Action Publishing,
<http://dx.doi.org/10.3362/9781788531405>

Since 1974, Practical Action Publishing has published and disseminated books and information in support of international development work throughout the world. Practical Action Publishing is a trading name of Practical Action Publishing Ltd (Company Reg. No. 1159018), the wholly owned publishing company of Practical Action. Practical Action Publishing trades only in support of its parent charity objectives and any profits are covenanted back to Practical Action (Charity Reg. No. 247257, Group VAT Registration No. 880 9924 76).

Editing: Erin Seatter
Design: John van der Woude, jvdw Designs
Printed on demand

Contents

To Sophia,
may your future be bright and full of opportunity

Critical Development Studies Series

Three decades of uneven capitalist development and neoliberal globalization have devastated the economies, societies, livelihoods and lives of people around the world, especially those in societies of the Global South. Now more than ever, there is a need for a more critical, proactive approach to the study of global and development studies. The challenge of advancing and disseminating such an approach — to provide global and development studies with a critical edge — is on the agenda of scholars and activists from across Canada and the world and those who share the concern and interest in effecting progressive change for a better world.

This series provides a forum for the publication of small books in the interdisciplinary field of critical development studies — to generate knowledge and ideas about transformative change and alternative development. The editors of the series welcome the submission of original manuscripts that focus on issues of concern to the growing worldwide community of activist scholars in this field. Critical development studies (CDS) encompasses a broad array of issues ranging from the sustainability of the environment and livelihoods, the political economy and sociology of social inequality, alternative models of local and community-based development, the land and resource-grabbing dynamics of extractive capital, the subnational and global dynamics of political and economic power, and the forces of social change and resistance, as well as the contours of contemporary struggles against the destructive operations and ravages of capitalism and imperialism in the twenty-first century.

The books in the series are designed to be accessible to an activist readership as well as the academic community. The intent is to publish a series of small books (54,000 words, including bibliography, endnotes, index and front matter) on some of the biggest issues in the interdisciplinary field of critical development studies. To this end, activist scholars from across the world in the field of development studies and related academic disciplines are invited to submit a proposal or the draft of a book that conforms to the stated aim of the series. The editors will consider the submission of complete manuscripts within the 54,000-word limit. Potential authors are encouraged to submit a proposal that includes a rationale and short synopsis of the book, an outline of proposed chapters, one or two sample chapters, and a brief biography of the author(s).

Series Editors

HENRY VELTMEYER is a research professor at Universidad Autónoma de Zacatecas (Mexico) and professor emeritus of International Development Studies at Saint Mary's University (Canada), with a specialized interest in Latin American development. He is also co-chair of the Critical Development Studies Network and a co-editor of Fernwood's Agrarian Change and Peasant Studies series. The *CDS Handbook: Tools for Change* (Fernwood, 2011) was published in French by University of Ottawa Press as *Des outils pour le changement : Une approche critique en études du développement* and in Spanish as *Herramientas para el Cambio*, with funding from Oxfam UK by CIDES, Universidad Mayor de San Andrés, La Paz, Bolivia.

ANNETTE AURÉLIE DESMARAIS is the Canada Research Chair in Human Rights, Social Justice and Food Sovereignty at the University of Manitoba (Canada). She is the author of *La Vía Campesina: Globalization and the Power of Peasants* (Fernwood, 2007), which has been republished in French, Spanish, Korean, Italian and Portuguese, and *Frontline Farmers: How the National Farmers Union Resists Agribusiness and Creates our New Food Future* (Fernwood, 2019). She is co-editor of *Food Sovereignty: Reconnecting Food, Nature and Community* (Fernwood, 2010); *Food Sovereignty in Canada: Creating Just and Sustainable Food Systems* (Fernwood, 2011); and *Public Policies for Food Sovereignty: Social Movements and the State* (Routledge, 2017).

RAÚL DELGADO WISE is a research professor and director of the PhD program in Development Studies at the Universidad Autónoma de Zacatecas (Mexico). He holds the prestigious UNESCO Chair on Migration and Development and is executive director of the International Migration and Development Network, as well as author and editor of some twenty books and more than a hundred essays. He is a member of the Mexican Academy of Sciences and editor of the book series, Latin America and the New World Order, for Miguel Angel Porrúa publishers and chief editor of the journal *Migración y Desarrollo*. He is also a member of the international working group, People's Global Action on Migration Development and Human Rights.

Foreword

This book brings to mind the *Open Veins of Latin America: Five Centuries of the Pillage of a Continent* by Eduardo Galeano. First published in 1971 the book became an instant classic, selling over a million copies worldwide. The novelist Isabel Allende even wrote a foreword for the 1997 edition. The book was written under the influence of dependency theory in both its structuralist and Marxist strands. The colonial exploitation of the riches of Latin America and their subsequent exploitation by national and foreign capital created an economic and social system which reproduced underdevelopment, poverty and dependence by transferring the continent's riches to the dominant countries. When governments in the region tried to gain control over their natural resources by reformist or revolutionary means they were often overthrown, as happened during the 1970s and 1980s when military dictatorships took control. They were often the harbingers, together with their civilian counterparts, of the neoliberal turn, which dismantled the developmentalist state with its protectionist industrial policies, agrarian reform programs and focus on the domestic market. The region once again extended its arms to foreign capital and shifted to an export oriented strategy based on the exploitation and export of raw materials.

Neoliberal policies led to a dramatic rise in poverty and inequality, provoking a backlash which brought into power left-wing social and political forces in several countries at the turn of the century in a movement known as the "pink tide." They gained power by promising a post-neoliberal agenda, taking back control over national resources, promoting equity, food sovereignty, social inclusion, rights for Indigenous Peoples and respect for Mother Nature. In recent years, the pink tide has been reversed in several countries as progressive governments were overthrown, often by dubious or illegal means. Evo Morales came to power in 2006 with the overwhelming support of various Indigenous social movements, becoming the country's first Indigenous president. His government greatly enhanced the rights of Indigenous Peoples as well as their dignity. It was able to take advantage of the commodities boom which allowed it to achieve major reductions in poverty. However, by furthering an extractivist development model it increasingly alienated and came into conflict with some social organizations which had supported it.

Bolivia has been throughout its history an extractivist economy being dependent on the rents it generated. Its veins were opened by colonialism exploiting the rich silver mines which oiled the world economy. Later, in the independence period, other minerals were also exported, such as tin and more recently hydrocarbons, all on the back of an exploited Indigenous labour force. The Movement Towards Socialism (MAS) government of Evo Morales promised a New Economic, Social, Communitarian and Productive Model as a post-neoliberal strategy of development. To achieve sustainable development this strategy aimed to develop an industrial sector so as to reduce its dependence on natural resource exports. In my view, the development strategy in Bolivia, although couched in a socialist rhetoric, was much influenced by the neostructuralist proposal of "changing production patterns with social equity" emanating from the Economic Commission for Latin America and the Caribbean (ECLAC) and associated development thinkers, some of whom had earlier contributed to the structuralist strand of dependency theory. This strategy sought to achieve "development from within" by making the productive structure less dependent on raw materials and cheap labour and, above all, by developing high value-added production processes and services and enhancing the qualifications, skills and competence of workers so as to raise productivity and thereby improve living standards and equity.

The extent to which the Morales government has been able to reduce the extractivist character of its economy is one of the key issues examined by this book, written from a critical political economy perspective and more specifically within critical agrarian studies. Ben McKay coins the term "agrarian extractivism" to characterize the dominant soy agro-industrial complex, which he examines in detail. He concludes that the "extractivist syndrome" still pervades the economy and society. Furthermore, it has been enhanced by the "commodities boom," which has tied the Bolivian economy further to the global system.

The question remains as to why it is so difficult to escape from the "extractivist imperative." Is it due to lack of political will or power by the Bolivian government, as well as by the other pink tide governments who failed to transform the productive matrix toward a high-value added economy? Or is it due to the global force of the extractivist imperative? Or is it because extractivism is an easier option for governments given the complexity of the task to achieve sustainable and equitable development and the longer time horizon it requires? Elucidating the economic, social and political circumstances at national and global levels which would make it possible to accomplish this complex and difficult task is a crucial challenge facing scholars, activists, social movements, governments and world organizations. The great merit of this book is that it provides a solid foundation for other researchers to explore these wider issues.

— *Cristóbal Kay*
The Hague, October 2019

Introduction: Agrarian Change and the Politics of Control

The global agro-food system is undergoing a geopolitical restructuring. Transnational capital is not only flowing through new geographies but also creating new spaces for capital to penetrate, circulate and accumulate. The political and economic rise of emerging economies such as the BRICS countries — Brazil, Russia, India, China and South Africa — and other middle-income countries combined with the recent convergence of crises around food prices, peak oil, finance and climate change have fuelled increasing demands for flex crops, commodities and investments in and around plantation agriculture. New hubs of global capital accumulation have surfaced, representing key sites of production, circulation and consumption that challenge existing conceptions of a North-South divide as the most significant dimension of global inequality in power and wealth (see McKay, Hall and Liu 2016). These changing global dynamics have important implications for agricultural sectors, rural livelihoods, food security, the environment and national development. Industrial value-chain agriculture has become the dominant model for rural development, expanding into new frontiers around the world and led by powerful corporations, international aid and development institutions and state actors as the way forward to alleviate rural poverty, feed the nearly one billion hungry people worldwide and keep up with a growing global population expected to reach 9.7 billion in 2050 (FAO, IFAD and WFP 2015; UN 2015).

Soybeans have been at the centre of these agrarian transformations as one of the world's most important crops in terms of land use, trade and production value, and as a quintessential flex crop with its multiple and flexible uses as food, feed, fuel and industrial materials (Oliveira and Schneider 2016). Soybean plantations have expanded and engulfed vast swaths of land across Latin America's Southern Cone, which includes Argentina, Bolivia, Brazil, Paraguay and Uruguay and is now the world's leading producer and exporter of the oilseed crop. In the Latin American context, the politics of land and agricultural development have become intricately tied to a global agro-industrial soy complex[1] with soybean expansion developing rapidly, yet unevenly, across the Southern Cone since the 1970s. New actors and forms of capital penetration in the countryside associated with the soy complex — and the rush for natural resources more generally — have prompted debates as to whether such rising global interests in farmland and agro-commodities represent threats or opportunities for rural development (Deininger and Byerlee 2011; Borras and Franco 2010). On the one hand, several pull factors have encouraged many peasants and small-scale farmers to cultivate genetically modified (GM) soybean monocultures, including a commodities boom that led to favourable soybean prices as well as discourses of modernization and progress. On the other hand, push factors such as soil contamination due to airplane fumigation and river run-off, unfavourable domestic market conditions and other economic and extra-economic forms of dispossession have forced many to either abandon their lands and migrate to urban areas, search for employment as wage labourers in rural areas, transition to capital-intensive agricultural production or engage in various combinations thereof.

These processes of agrarian change are not unique to soybean production; they are common to agro-industrial expansion throughout the world. Dominant discourses based on the need to feed a growing population, to end rural poverty and provide opportunities for the rural poor to escape the drudgery of peasant farming, to modernize production by engineering seeds that can produce in abundance on less favourable soil and climatic conditions are widespread and continue to shape the official policy agendas of international development institutions and national governments. This book engages with these debates and challenges such dominant discourses through an investigation of the politics and processes of agrarian change in the context of the development and expansion of the agro-industrial soy complex in Bolivia.

Perhaps better known as a producer of quinoa and coca — and for its progressive political regime formerly headed by the country's first Indigenous president, Evo Morales, and the Movement Towards Socialism (Movimiento al Socialismo, MAS), which assumed state power in 2006 and was forced in to resign in November 2019 due to widespread social pressure — Bolivia is one of the top ten soybean producers in the world. Soybeans have become the country's principal agricultural crop, one of its top three exports and a pillar of its three-pronged extractivist development model along with minerals and hydrocarbons. The oilseed crop has transformed the country's landscape, replacing traditional crops and forested lands, and has significantly changed the forms and relations of production, property and power. In the context of a changing international political economy of food and agriculture, this book investigates the ways in which the development and expansion of the agro-industrial soy complex in Bolivia are transforming agrarian social relations in the eastern lowlands of Santa Cruz, including the diverse socioeconomic and environmental implications and the politics behind these processes. The particularities of agro-industry's penetration into Bolivia have significant implications for rural development and can serve to illuminate broader understandings of agro-industrial development more generally.

This book reveals how mechanized soybean production in Bolivia has developed similar to an extractive enclave, socially and sectorally disarticulated from the rest of the economy with production destined for export markets. Labour has become surplus to the needs of capital accumulation in the soy complex, and since the oilseed flex crop is sold to external markets there is no need for agro-industry to be concerned with domestic consumer capacity or a robust internal market. Many small farmers have limited access to land and capital and little opportunity for upward mobility, yet they become caught in contradictory class positions, permitting a functional dualism in the countryside in which the development and expansion of the agro-industrial soy complex is relatively unchallenged socially and politically despite its exclusionary and extractivist characteristics.

This book addresses aspects of the contemporary agrarian questions of capital and labour by asking not if capital is penetrating the countryside, but how and to what extent agro-industrial capital is developing in the countryside, as well as about the new forms (of control) it has taken in terms of shaping relations of production and accumulation and the political formations associated with these processes (Byres 1986, 1996; Bernstein 1996). How and to what extent new forms of capital are penetrating the countryside and their implications for agrarian transformation remain important for national development and poverty alleviation and remain underexplored and insufficiently explained in the literature. Studies that analyze soybean expansion and agrarian change in Santa Cruz provide excellent insights into the functioning of land markets, land concentration, foreignization and technological transfer (Colque 2014; Mackey 2011; Urioste 2012; Zoomers 2003), but do not engage with the new forms of control that have emerged in the context of capital-intensive and highly mechanized value-chain agriculture in Bolivia.

Dominant discourses from the state, international institutions such as the World Bank and the soybean sector present alternative explanations of the implications of this new capital penetration in the countryside based on economic growth, productivity, food security and sovereignty and employment generation (Vicepresidente 2012; IBCE 2014). This book challenges these claims, arguing that a deeper understanding of the social relations of production reveals very exclusionary dynamics, the appropriation of the surplus value by a concentrated market oligopoly and the extractive character of agricultural production. Analyzing dynamics of agrarian change using a property rights–based framework, or aggregate productivity levels and export-revenue generation, fails to capture these dynamics of control, exclusion, value appropriation and extraction that are central to this analysis and are further elaborated on in the context of the new dynamics of agrarian change in Bolivia.

The Politics of Control: An Analytical Framework

New forms and mechanisms of capital penetration in the countryside require us to go beyond a framework based on property rights or formal land ownership to one of control grabbing. For Borras et al. (2012: 850), "control grabbing is inherently relational and political; it involves political power relations" and can manifest in a variety of ways that do "not always result in dispossession." The analytical framework that guides this book, referred to as the politics of control, builds upon this concept and synthesizes three other theoretical interventions: (1) Ribot and Peluso's (2003) "theory of access" and the new forms and mechanisms of control that have emerged in (agro) extractive development; (2) the works of O'Connor (1973), Poulantzas (1978) and Jessop (2008) on the nature and role of the capitalist state; and (3) the works of Fox (1993) and Borras (2007) on state-society relations. The analytical utility of the politics of control are twofold: First, it captures the new forms and mechanisms of resource control and value appropriation (or extraction) in (agro)extractive sectors through an analysis of access rather than property or concessional rights. These include various forms of dispossession and displacement, but also mechanisms of exclusion and appropriation that do not necessarily require the physical removal of people from the land. Second, it provides a framework for analyzing the state's dual and often contradictory functions of facilitating capital accumulation and maintaining political legitimacy and the strategic relations between state and societal actors in gaining and maintaining control over the state apparatus. Control therefore has a dual meaning: control over the state apparatus and control over the factors of production (land, labour, capital) and thus resource access. Several concepts are developed throughout this work that help us understand the politics of control, such as productive exclusion, value-chain control, agrarian extractivism and state-society-capital nexus.

In the state-society relations literature, variants of state- and society-centred approaches provide explanatory frameworks for state action, policy outcomes and socioeconomic change. Some of these approaches tend to understand the state and society as mutually exclusive and self-determining entities that can be analyzed in isolation, with "clear and unambiguous boundaries between state apparatus and society, state managers and social forces, and state power and societal power" (Jessop 2008:155). This implies that we can understand the workings of the state without necessarily understanding society or the societal structure and vice versa, ruling out "hybrid logics such as corporatism or policy networks; divisions among state managers due to ties between state organs and other social spheres; and many other forms of overlaps between state and society" (Jessop 2008: 155). However, while the state and society may appear to be two separate entities, they are inextricably linked as a relation, and thus we cannot understand the workings of the state apparatus, its institutions and state managers without understanding the social structure that makes up society.

When we consider the relations between state and societal actors concerning "revolving door politics," when banks are too big to fail or when lobby groups or key constituents are highly influential in electoral politics, the apparent lines between the state and society become increasingly blurred. Even within the state apparatus, state managers (elected and appointed) are increasingly at odds with one another as politics becomes ever more polarizing. As Wolford and French (2016: 11) point out, "Just as civil society actors struggle for access to state resources, so, too, state agencies and employees have to negotiate and struggle for recognition and resources against competitors within the government apparatus." In Bolivia, relations between Morales and opposition leader and governor of Santa Cruz Rubén Costas went from the latter calling the former an "assassin" and a "dictator" and threatening a coup in 2008 to an apparent alliance in 2013–14 (*Economía Bolivia* 2013; Ortiz 2013). Morales was then invited to meetings with associations representing agro-industry such as the Agricultural Chamber of Eastern Bolivia (Camara Agropecuaria del Oriente), the Santa Cruz Chamber of Industry, Commerce, Services and Tourism (Cámara de Industria, Comercio, Servicios y Turismo de Santa Cruz) and the National Association of Producers of Oilseeds and Wheat (Asociación Nacional de

Productores de Oleaginosas y Trigo, ANAPO) and inaugurated corporate events of the Santa Cruz elite such as Fexpocruz and Expo Soya. How do we understand this state-capital alliance?

With the wave of progressive left governments across the Latin American region taking power in the first decade of the 2000s, scholars have sought to re-engage with, and challenge, the notion of a separation between the state and society (Cannon and Kirby 2012; Wolford and French 2016). Cannon and Kirby (2012: 202) contend that there is a "dialectical nature of state, civil society and market relations" that must be understood as a co-constitutive unified whole rather than analyzed separately. Drawing on Fraser's (1990) concept of strong publics, these authors suggest that "the role of civil society has moved beyond mere opinion formation to involvement ... in the making of decisions" (Cannon and Kirby 2012: 202). This could certainly be argued in Bolivia as movements from the Pacto de Unidad[2] form part of the National Coordination for Change (Coordinadora Nacional para el Cambio)[3] and the Constituent Assembly responsible for designing and implementing the 2009 Constitution. However, as Schilling-Vacaflor and Vollrath (2012: 137) argue, despite the discursive and apparent inclusion of Bolivian civil society in decision-making, their opinions "tend to be overridden by governmental priorities" based on extractivism. In Argentina, Wylde (2012: 46) argues, despite the disappearance and state co-optation of the more radical forms of resistance that emerged from the economic crisis of 2001–02, it "nevertheless led to important and lasting changes in the Argentine social contract owing more widely to the absorption of many of the ideas of these movements into state policy."

This book contributes to this literature and understands social and political change by engaging with the state and society not as independent variables but as a historically situated strategic social relation that is always in motion, shaped and reshaped by their respective actors and institutions in specific conjunctures. The state apparatus is thus understood not as a fully autonomous entity or an instrument of the capitalist class but as a terrain of contested and strategic relations among political forces attempting to appear neutral and "outside" of the society. As an ensemble of unequal power centres activated through the agency of state managers and their interaction with specific social forces, state power is maintained through a fine balance of facilitating capital accumulation and maintaining legitimacy by reconciling class conflict and antagonisms within and between classes of capital and labour (Jessop 2008; O'Connor 1973).

Capital accumulation and legitimacy, as O'Connor (1973: 6) puts it, are "two basic and often mutually contradictory functions" of the capitalist state. Agencies of the state can exercise their power in order to encourage and facilitate capital accumulation through fiscal and monetary policy, trade agreements, subsidies, infrastructure investment and so on to increase the state's fiscal capacity, which "depends upon revenues that originate in the sphere of production" (de Janvry 1981: 196). Conversely, in order to maintain legitimacy, state institutions and agents must create the conditions for social harmony and reconcile conflicting class interests in society. This manifests in a variety of forms such as social welfare programs, a progressive income tax system, increased social and environmental regulations, redistributive reforms, public education and healthcare, social security and unemployment insurance and forms of strategic popular discourse. However, agencies of the state do not exercise their power and effect change just as they please; they must interact (often strategically) with the balance of forces in society.

If state expenditures surpass fiscal revenues in order to increase political legitimacy (through the redistribution of extractive rents, for example), the state risks entering into a fiscal crisis (O'Connor 1973). However, if the state facilitates capital accumulation beyond its legitimacy threshold without social, environmental and financial regulations — to the point where it facilitates capital accumulation at the expense of the welfare of the masses — it risks a crisis of legitimacy and financial crises. Crises can lead to political reforms, social revolution, political coups or repressive forms of control by the state. The extent to which the agencies of the state pursue legitimating and accumulation strategies is politically contingent on external demands, the autonomy and capacity of state actors and "the nature of their interaction with contending forces making those demands" (Fox 1993: 31). The formulation of government policies and legislation is always a contested process, and even when they are drawn up on paper, they do not self-interpret or self-implement; they are shaped, interpreted and implemented according to the very political interactions between state and societal actors (Franco 2008).

For purposes of conceptual clarity, I categorize the interests of the various social classes and class fractions with which state managers must interact as those who represent classes of labour[4] (representing society in the state-society-capital nexus), having political and economic interests in the subjective function of the state, and those which represent classes of capital[5] (representing capital in the state-society-capital nexus), having political and economic interests in the objective function of the state.[6] Although there are certainly other class fractions and transitional classes such as semiproletarians and petty bourgeoisie that at times are in contradictory class positions, their socioeconomic and political interests are influenced by this principal contradiction — that is, between labour and capital, or the interests of the proletariat and the bourgeoisie. Using the conceptual framework referred to here as the state-society-capital nexus can provide a clearer understanding of the complex web of relations that leads to social and political change. As an approach to understanding the nature of the state, the state-society-capital nexus does not separate the economic from the political and thus reduce state action and sociopolitical change to either economic or political determinism. Rather, it treats the relation of the economic and political as inherently embedded within social relations under capitalism.

The state-society-capital nexus provides a framework of analysis to understand the nature of the state through the capital relation — that is, a relation of class struggle between classes of labour and capital. The capital relation assumes two forms, the economic and the political;[7] state managers must therefore maintain the organization of the capitalist process of production, appear as a neutral entity outside of society and reconcile class differences of labour and capital through balancing capital accumulation and legitimacy. Throughout this book, the politics of agrarian change in Bolivia are analyzed through the lens of the state-society-capital nexus to contribute to a better understanding of the social and political change that has taken place since the election of Evo Morales and MAS in 2006.

Agrarian Dynamics in Bolivia: A Brief Overview

Bolivia's agrarian structure is highly unequal. After undergoing two agrarian reform programs — following the 1952 revolution, which overthrew the military junta headed by General Hugo Ballivián and brought the leftist Revolutionary Nationalist Movement (Movimiento Nacionalista Revolucionario, MNR) to power, and then a so-called "agrarian revolution" in 2006 — the country's rural sector remains characterized by an extremely unequal landholding structure. Of the roughly 860,000 farm units in the country, 91 percent are small farms[8] occupying just 14 percent of the total available arable land (INE 2015). The country has one of the highest rural-urban ratios in Latin America with 33.5 percent of the total population living in rural areas and almost one-third (29.1 percent) of the total workforce employed in agriculture (INE 2012). Land-based wealth and agriculture as a livelihood and economic activity are therefore still very relevant and extremely important for poverty alleviation and rural development (IFAD 2010). However, the policies and programs pursued by governments over the last sixty years have led to a rigid and entrenched agrarian structure in which classes of landholding and capitalist elites (classes of capital) have gained and maintained access and control over the majority of the country's most fertile land and productive resources. These inequalities coincide with a severe poverty rate of over two-thirds (66.4 percent) of the rural population, while nearly half of all rural people live in extreme poverty (45.5 percent) (INE 2012).

While Bolivia's current agrarian structure has been shaped by previous sociopolitical periods that generated patterns of dispossession and land concentration, changes in the global political economy are resulting in new forms of capital penetration with new mechanisms of exclusion, value appropriation and extraction associated with the agro-industrial soy complex. This model of agro-industrial production and the development of new biotechnologies transformed the region into the world's leading producer of soybeans, with Brazil leading the way by spreading its technologies and producers throughout Latin America's Southern Cone (Oliveira and Hecht 2016).

To date, a limited number of studies exist on issues related to the new agrarian dynamics in Bolivia in the context of the recent penetration of new agro-capitals and the soy complex. Studies have analyzed the workings of Bolivia's land markets (Zoomers 2003) and land appropriation on the frontier (Colque 2014), while others have focused on the foreignization of land as Brazilian capitalist farmers and agro-industry increase their presence and control over Bolivia's land-based natural resources (Urioste 2012; Mackey 2011). These works have provided valuable insights and contributed to understandings of agrarian change in Bolivia, providing the basis from which this study takes off. Building on these and other works, this book attempts to go beyond a land-centric and foreignization lens to reveal the hidden forms and mechanisms of exclusion, control, appropriation and extraction and the politics behind these processes.

During the last twenty years, foreigners — specifically Brazilians — have rapidly increased their control over Bolivian agricultural land and resources. In 2006–07, for example, Brazilians controlled 40.3 percent of total soy plantation area in Bolivia, up from 19.6 percent in 1994–95 (Urioste 2012). Although there is no available data on the total amount of land controlled by Brazilians at present, the most reliable and recent study, conducted by Miguel Urioste (2012: 449) of Fundación TIERRA, suggests that

> in oilseeds alone, Brazilians own approximately half a million hectares of the best agricultural lands, both category I (intensive agricultural use) and category II (extensive agricultural use), without counting

those that are in fallow or rotation, nor those that are directed towards other crops or ranching, which usually comprise larger areas.

Urioste (2012) also suggests that the more recent investments from Brazilians in Bolivia are in pasture lands for cattle ranching, estimating that Brazilian cattle ranchers occupy 700,000 hectares in the three provinces bordering Brazil (German Busch, Velasco and Angel Sandoval) within the Department of Santa Cruz. Brazilian capital therefore controls an estimated 1.2 million hectares of Bolivia's 2.86 million hectares of cultivated land, with Brazilian-based corporations Grupo Monica (Monica Semillas), Gama Group and UNISOYA controlling over 200,000 hectares of this land (Urioste 2012). However, the data is very much outdated, and with the state's land titling process (*saneamiento*)[9] still incomplete and ANAPO unwilling to release specific data on its members, land concentration and so-called foreignization could be much higher than these figures reveal. Based on discussions with key informants working in the municipal governments of Cuatro Cañadas and San Julián — the two main communities in the soybean expansion zone — as well as numerous small farmers, it is clear that a culture of illegal land appropriation and land-grabbing continues in the eastern lowlands.

Urioste's data, for example, is based on reports published by ANAPO, Bolivia's politically and economically influential association of large-scale agro-industrialists, which aims to reproduce the Brazilian model of agriculture in Bolivia. ANAPO has access to the most accurate information regarding land tenure (and nationality) since its members report this data to the association. However, ANAPO's publications in recent years no longer include specific information on producer nationality, largely due to publications released by a Bolivian NGO on the issue of foreign land grabs. According to Rodolfo Machaca, leader of the Unified Confederation of Peasants of Bolivia (Confederación Sindical Única de Trabajadores Campesinos de Bolivia), ANAPO's publications led to a public backlash against ANAPO not only from its members but also from the public at large, and especially rural worker and peasant associations that only recently put the issue of the foreignization of land on their political agenda. It is clear that ANAPO values and encourages foreign investment, especially from Brazil. According to ANAPO's president in 2014, Demetrio Perez, investment from Brazil, Argentina and other countries has helped and continues to modernize Bolivia's soy sector with new machinery, seed and agro-chemical technologies, expertise and highway development. Urioste (2012: 446) also points out that "two of the leading Brazilian soybean producers serve on the board of ANAPO, even though this requires changes to organizational statutes." ANAPO's agenda is clearly to support the development and expansion of agro-industry for export, representing those medium- and large-scale farmers (22 percent of total farm units) who control 90 percent of the cultivated soybean area in Bolivia (ANAPO 2011). Urioste (2012: 450) also suggests a general acceptance of the foreign presence — especially among the middle classes of Santa Cruz — so as to secure access to "sources of capital, technology, employment, business, market knowledge, inputs and genetically-modified seeds."

This general acceptance is similar to Mackey's (2011) research findings in the region, which give primacy to Brazilian technological transfer in manufacturing consent among Bolivian farmers. Like Urioste, Mackey points to the use of technology as a terrain of legitimation and the informal class alliances among Bolivian and Brazilian agro-industrialists that have led to the foreignization of Bolivia's eastern lowlands. Mackey suggests that it is important to consider the Brazilian presence in Bolivia in terms of the much broader political economic relationships between the two countries and Brazil's position as a regional hegemon and alternative to western imperialism. Brazil's role in the production and consumption of the Bolivian hydrocarbon sector, as well its role as a leading creditor, primarily for transportation infrastructure but also for agricultural machinery, has solidified bilateral relations between the countries and led to a general acceptance of Brazilians in Bolivia (Mackey 2011). According to Brazil's foreign minister of economic affairs in South America, Joao Parkinson de Castro, the ministry always prefers to avoid any discourse regarding Brazilians in Bolivia, but they do support their citizens across the border through political negotiation if necessary. The minister told me in 2014 that the relationship with the Bolivian government was delicate but positive and that the Brazilians always "want to avoid any discourses of regional imperialism." He added that "the economic relationship between Santa Cruz and Mato Grosso/Mato Grosso do Sul is very important, but the politics in La Paz can sometimes threaten this relationship, so it is important that our government supports but does not overextend its influence in Bolivia."

Colque (2014) reveals the workings of land appropriation on the frontier in Santa Cruz, focusing on the concentration of land-based wealth and power held among agro-industrial elites and their ability to challenge and dispute the authority of the state. Colque traces these land-based power relations through several stages of appropriation dating back to the country's first agrarian reform in 1953. Appropriation of land, he argues, predominantly occurs through informal and illegal land deals that exploit and further marginalize the rural poor.

Redo, Millington and Hindery (2011: 235) document the dynamics of deforestation in the lowlands of Santa Cruz, suggesting that "most (of the deforestation) resulted from Brazilian farmers and ranchers moving into the north-east of the region from Mato Grosso do Sul." This study and others have brought to light the important and contested issue of the foreign (mainly Brazilian) presence in Bolivia's eastern lowlands. It is clear that foreigners, especially Brazilians, have come to control a large share of agricultural land in Bolivia over the past three decades. But what is of interest here is not only if and how foreigners are controlling large parcels of land in Bolivia but more importantly how new forms and mechanisms of capital investment are changing relations of production, property and power; who is appropriating the value generated by this agro-industrial expansion; and the implications and trajectories of this type of agrarian change. Changes in the agrarian political economy, even where foreign capital is present, cannot be fully captured using a foreignization lens. Similarly, an overly land-centric focus can lose sight of relations of debt, dependency and exclusion whereby land and resource control shift without physical displacement or property rights–based changes.

The focus on nationality presents a veiled threat to understanding the nature, pace and trajectories of agrarian change in the broader context of new forms and mechanisms of control. The lines distinguishing national from trans-Latin capital have become increasingly blurred as joint ventures, subsidiaries, informal partnerships, land leasing, financing and cross-border marriages render it increasingly difficult to distinguish between Bolivian and Brazilian capital in many instances. Nationality should become central if it leads to capital flight, but not necessarily if it operates similarly to domestic capital. As the national origins of capital and financial investment become intertwined, it becomes more important to reveal the changing relations of access and control over land and resources and the politics behind these processes. This book therefore does not analyze the new processes of agrarian restructuring in Bolivia as foreignization, but rather in terms of the logic of capital and its incessant drive for accumulation through expanded reproduction, dispossession and exclusion. Breaking down imaginary national borders and giving primacy to the classes of capital "distinguished by the interest and strategies of capital in particular activities and sectors and on scales from local to regional, national to transnational" (Bernstein 2010: 112) requires going beyond the "foreignization of property" to the "*character* and *direction* of change in social relations of property" (Borras et al. 2012: 864; emphasis in original). These dynamics of agrarian change are analyzed in two communities at the heart of Bolivia's soybean expansion zone: Cuatro Cañadas and San Julián.

Cuatro Cañadas and San Julián lie at the centre of Bolivia's soybean expansion zone and are located about 100 kilometres east of the country's most populated and fastest-growing city of Santa Cruz de la Sierra. They developed as a direct result of planned migratory policies and the arrival of Mennonites, who established their colonies in the area and were pioneers of the frontier expansion. While Mennonites purchased vast swaths of land known as colonies, which today are an average size of 11,000 hectares divided into family parcels of 50 hectares, highland peasants were given plots of up to 50 hectares each by the government. Cuatro Cañadas and San Julián have experienced the most rapid rates of land use change over the past two decades and continue to be key sites of agro-industrial expansion, accounting for nearly 50 percent of the country's total soybean output. Economic and demographic flows correlate with the soybean sector. During periods of harvest, the towns are bustling as massive transport trucks, tractors and harvesters move from parcel to parcel, village to village, collecting soybean grains for storage, processing and export. The heavy traffic generates giant dust clouds, which swallow up the town and the municipality's three hotels, and the few restaurants overflow with people, as local businesses earn the majority of their annual revenue during periods of harvest. The region's fertile lands produce two harvests per year, though the summer season is the most favourable for soybean cultivation and farmers usually cultivate maize, sunflower, sorghum or wheat in the winter harvest (Álvarez Álvarez 2005; Gobierno Municipal de Cuatro Cañadas 2008). Indeed, the municipalities Cuatro Cañadas and San Julián are the product of the agro-industrial soy complex. This region is the boundary of Bolivia's agricultural frontier, which continues to expand, coinciding with Indigenous territories and classes of rural labour vying for land access.

These communities do not exist in a vacuum and are analyzed in the context of geopolitical relations with neighbouring Brazil and broader socio-economic and political dynamics at the national, regional and international levels. While offering intrinsic value and relational specificity at the micro level, at the macro level the case study is used in an instrumental way to provide more generalizable analytical insights and theoretical explanations. The book therefore seeks to draw insights from these case studies on a much broader scale. The empirical data collected from nearly one hundred key informant interviews,[10] countless informal conversations and a survey of over three hundred households illuminates the more generalizable trends and tendencies of agro-industrial capital's penetration into the countryside in the contemporary era. Using data triangulation through a mixed methods approach, this study draws empirical generalizations about the larger group of producers and smallholders integrated in the soy complex. Analytical generalizations are also drawn from the exclusionary and extractive tendencies of the soy complex and agro-capital penetration more broadly. Such insights and analyses can contribute to new understandings of agrarian questions and the politics of agrarian change in the contemporary period.

Organization of the Argument

This book consists of seven chapters, including this introduction and a conclusion. Chapter 1 discusses the development of the soy complex in Latin America, from the commercialization of GM soybean seeds to agrochemicals, processing and distribution. It proceeds with an overview of the emergence of a market oligopoly controlling the upstream and downstream components of soybean production and the importance of Brazil in adopting, developing and transferring technologies and its agro-industrial model throughout the region. The combination of a changing global political economy of food and agriculture and biotechnology innovations fuelled the expansion of soybean plantations on a great scale, triggering a trajectory of agrarian change throughout the region that has had important and lasting implications for agricultural development and geopolitical relations.

In Chapter 2, the development of Bolivia's agrarian structure is analyzed historically through several phases of transition — revolution, migration, crises and agrarian reforms. The expansion of the agricultural frontier and the arrival of Brazilian agro-capitalists is discussed with firsthand experiences from some of the first Brazilian farmers who went to Santa Cruz in the 1990s. Relations between state, societal and capitalist actors and the forms of legitimacy and accumulation that characterize these periods are analyzed within the politics of control framework. The emergence of new social movements and the rejection of neoliberalism set the conditions for the rise of Evo Morales and MAS as a "government of social movements."

Chapter 3 analyzes the politics of agrarian change during the Morales administration, from its agrarian revolution in 2006 to the productive revolution in 2011. The state-society-capital nexus is analyzed within this changing context, and I argue that a state-capital alliance was formed that enabled MAS to maintain control over the state apparatus, and the classes of capital in Santa Cruz to maintain control over the soy complex. New forms of exclusion and mechanisms of control that place smallholders in contradictory class positions have led to a functional dualism in the countryside, hindering the ability of smallholders to mobilize and organize as a "class for itself" and voice demands to the state.

Chapter 4 takes a step back to focus on the forms of value appropriation via value-chain control and relations of debt and dependency. The chapter reveals the limited value added that is generated by the sector as agro-industrial inputs are imported from abroad and the soybean, only semiprocessed, is exported for further processing elsewhere. The concentration of control over the entire complex points to limited competition as corporations distort prices and heavily influence quality standards and input requirements. Institutional arrangements of debt and dependency are revealed, eroding farmer knowledge and their control over production.

The concept of agrarian extractivism is further developed in Chapter 5. This chapter reveals the very extractive character of the agro-industrial soy complex. Four key interlinked features of agrarian extractivism in Bolivia are put forth: (1) significant volumes of raw materials exports, (2) value-chain concentration and sectoral disarticulation, (3) high intensity of environmental degradation, and (4) deterioration of labour opportunities, labour conditions, or both. I argue here that this type of agro-industrial development parallels that of an extractive enclave, disconnected from sufficient value added and employment-generation activity due to a lack of forward and backward linkages with the rest of the economy with a high intensity of environmental degradation. Agrarian extractivism challenges legitimating discourses of industrial agriculture, highlighting the need to delve analytically into its extractive dynamics.

The conclusion provides a synthesis of the main findings of the book, including the analytical utility of the politics of control, the rise and influence of Brazilians in Bolivia's soy complex and the importance of using an analysis of access, control and exclusion rather than rights-based approaches. Based on the book's findings, some trajectories of agrarian change are discussed with broader implications for researchers, policymakers and social movements.

NOTES

1. This includes both upstream (seeds, land, agro-inputs, machinery) and downstream (storage, processing, packaging, distribution) components of soybean production, consumption and distribution.
2. The Pacto de Unidad (Unity Pact) is a social movement alliance formally convened in 2004 consisting of peasants (Unified Confederation of Peasants of Bolivia), intercultural communities (Syndicalist Confederation of Intercultural Communities of Bolivia), Indigenous, peasant and *originario* women (Bartolina Sisa National Confederation of Campesino, Indigenous, and Native Women of Bolivia) and Indigenous Peoples (Confederation of Indigenous Peoples of

Bolivia; National Council of Ayllus and Markas of Qullasuyu).

3. The National Coordination for Change is a political coordination of over twenty social movements in Bolivia aligned with MAS.
4. These include wage labourers, semiproletarians, and more generally those who "depend — directly and indirectly — on the sale of their labour power for their own daily reproduction" (Bernstein 2009: 73).
5. These include capitalist farmers, agro-industrialists, medium and large-scale landowners and more generally those who own and control the means of production.
6. De Janvry (1981) refers to the subjective and objective functions of the state as legitimization and accumulation, respectively. Though often contradictory, these functions are not mutually exclusive and can overlap. Policies such as financial deregulation, privatization of public institutions (e.g., healthcare) and trade liberalization may be considered as facilitating increased capital accumulation and therefore represent the objective function, while social services, public healthcare, cash transfers, old-age pensions, and so on may be considered as more favourable to classes of labour (thus reconciling class antagonisms) and therefore represent the subjective function.
7. The state apparatus represents the institutional and political expression of the capital relation which appears as an autonomous entity, yet has the legitimacy to reinforce contracts, regulations, and other processes which represent the economic form of the capitalist relation.
8. According to Law 3545 (*Reconducción de la reforma agraria*) established in 2006, in Santa Cruz small farms are defined as those with less than 50 hectares; medium-scale farms range from 51 to 500 hectares; and large-scale farms have over 500 hectares.
9. *Saneamiento* is a process of land regularization formalizing tenure relations.
10. Interviews were conducted in 2014 and 2015 with academics, researchers, social movement leaders, government officials, farmers, rural wage labourers, agro-industrial workers, transport truck and taxi drivers, agronomists and agricultural engineers.

REFERENCES

Álvarez Álvarez, Nataniel. 2005. *Cuatro Cañadas: Tierra y Desarrollo Rural*. La Paz: Fundación TIERRA.

ANAPO. 2011. *Memoria Anual 2011*. Santa Cruz: Asociacion de productores de oleaginosas y trigo.

Bernstein, Henry. 1996. "Agrarian Questions Then and Now." *The Journal of Peasant Studies*, 24 (1–2): 22–59.

____. 2009. "V.I. Lenin and A.V. Chayanov: Looking Back, Looking Forward." *Journal of Peasant Studies*, 36, 1: 55–81.

____. 2010. *Class Dynamics of Agrarian Change*. Halifax and Winnipeg: Fernwood Publishing.

Borras, Saturnino M. Jr. 2007. *Pro-Poor Land Reform: A Critique*. Ottawa: University of Ottawa Press.

Borras, Saturnino M. Jr., and Jennifer Franco. 2010. "From Threat to Opportunity? Problems with the Idea of a 'Code of Conduct' for Land-Grabbing." *Yale Human Rights & Development L.J.,* 13: 507–523.

Borras, Saturnino M. Jr., Jennifer C. Franco, Sergio Gomez, Cristóbal Kay, and Max Spoor. 2012. "Land Grabbing in Latin America and the Caribbean." *Journal of Peasant Studies,* 39, 3–4: 845–872.

Byres, T.J. 1986. "The Agrarian Question, Forms of Capitalist Agrarian Transition and the State: An Essay with Reference to Asia." *Social Scientist,* 14, 11/12: 3–67.

____. 1996. *Capitalism from Above and Capitalism from Below: An Essay in Comparative Political Economy*. UK: Palgrave Macmillan.

Cannon, Barry, and Kirby, Peadar. 2012. *Civil Society and the State in Left-Led Latin America: Challenges and Limitations to Democratization.* London and New York: Zed Books.

Colque, Gonzalo. 2014. *Expanión de La Frontera Agrícola: Luchas Por El Control y Apropiación de La Tierraen El Oriente Boliviano*. La Paz: Fundación TIERRA.

de Janvry, Alain. 1981. *The Agrarian Question and Reformism in Latin America.* Baltimore: Johns Hopkins University Press.

Deininger, Klaus, and Derek Byerlee. 2011. *Rising Global Interest in Farmland: Can It Yield Sustainable and Equitable Benefits?* Washington: World Bank.

Economía Bolivia. 2013. "Evo Morales Inaugurará La Expocruz Y El MAS Acelera Alianzas Con El Empresariado Cruceño Con Miras a 2014." <economiabolivia.org/2013/09/14/evo-morales-inaugurara-la-expocruz-el-mas-acelera-alianzas-con-el-empresariado-cruceno-con-miras-2014>

FAO, IFAD, and WFP. 2015. *The State of Food Insecurity in the World: Meeting the 2015 International Hunger Targets: Taking Stock of Uneven Progress. FAO, IFAD and WFP.*

Fox, Jonathan. 1993. *The Politics of Food in Mexico*. Ithaca and London: Cornell University Press.

Franco, Jennifer C. 2008. "Making Land Rights Accessible: Social Movements and Political-Legal Innovation in the Rural Philippines." *Journal of Development Studies,* 44, 7: 991–1022.

Fraser, Nancy. 1990. "Rethinking the Public Sphere: A Contribution to the Critique of Actually Existing Democracy." *Social Text,* 25/26: 56–80.

Gobierno Municipal de Cuatro Cañadas. 2008. "Plan Municipal de Ordenamiento Territorial." Cuatro Cañadas: Prefectura de Cuatro Cañadas.

IBCE. 2014. *Soya : Su Importancia Como Cadena de Valor Agroproductiva En Bolivia.* Vol. 227. Santa Cruz: Instituto Boliviano de Comercio Exterior.

IFAD (International Fund for Agricultural Development). 2010. *Rural Poverty Report 2011*. Rome: IFAD.

INE. 2012. "Información Estadística." *Instituto Nacional de Estadística.*

____. 2015. *Censo Agropecuario 2013*. La Paz: Instituto Nacional de Estadística.

Jessop, Bob. 2008. *State Power: A Strategic-Relational Approach. Statewide Agricultural Land Use Baseline 2015*. Vol. 1. Cambridge: Polity Press.

Mackey, L. 2011. "Legitimating Foreignization in Bolivia: Brazilian Agriculture and the Relations of Conflict and Consent in Santa Cruz, Bolivia. A Paper Presented at the Land." *International Conference on Global Land Grabbing,* April.

McKay, Ben M., Ruth Hall, and Juan Liu. 2016. "The Rise of BRICS : Implications for Global Agrarian Transformation." *Third World Thematics: A TWQ Journal,* 1, 5. Routledge: 581–591.

O'Connor, James. 1973. *The Fiscal Crisis of the State.* New York: St. Martin's Press.

Oliveira, Gustavo de L.T., and Susanna Hecht. 2016. "Sacred Groves, Sacrifice Zones and Soy Production: Globalization, Intensification and Neo-Nature in South America." *The Journal of Peasant Studies,* 43, 2: 251–285.

Oliveira, Gustavo de L.T., and Mindi Schneider. 2016. "The Politics of Flexing Soybeans: China, Brazil and Global Agroindustrial Restructuring." *The Journal of Peasant Studies,* 43, 1: 167–194.

Ortiz, Pablo. 2013. "Evo Morales: 'Estoy Contento, Siento Que El Cambio Llegó a Santa Cruz.'" *El Deber,* September 24.

Poulantzas, Nicos. 1978. *State, Power, Socialism.* London: Verso.

Redo, Daniel, Andrew C. Millington, and Derrick Hindery. 2011. "Deforestation Dynamics and Policy Changes in Bolivia's Post-Neoliberal Era." *Land Use Policy,* 28, 1: 227–241.

Ribot, Jesse C., and Nancy Lee Peluso. 2003. "A Theory of Access." *Rural Sociology,* 68, 2: 153–181.

Schilling-Vacaflor, Almut, and David Vollrath. 2012. "Indigenous and Peasant Participation in Resource Governance in Bolivia and Peru." In Barry Cannon and Peadar Kirby (eds.), *Civil Society and the State in Left-Led Latin America: Challenges and Limitations to Democratization.* London and New York: Zed Books.

UN. 2015. *World Population Prospects. United Nations.* Vol. 1. New York: United Nations.

Urioste, Miguel. 2012. "Concentration and 'Foreignisation' of Land in Bolivia." *Canadian Journal of Development Studies/Revue Canadienne d'études Du Développement,* 33, 4: 439–457.

Vicepresidente. 2012. "Gobierno y CAO Acuerdan Ampliar La Frontera Agricola Para Garantizar Soberanía Alimentaria." *Vicepresidencia Del Estado Plurinacional de Bolivia.*

Wolford, Wendy, and John D. French. 2016. "Introduction: Deconstructing the Post-Neoliberal State: Intimate Perspectives on Contemporary Brazil." *Latin American Perspectives* 43, 2: 4–21.

Wylde, Christopher. 2012. "State-Civil Society Relations in Post-Crisis Argentina." In Barry Cannon and Peadar Kirby (eds.), *Civil Society and the State in Left-Led Latin America: Challenges and Limitations to Democratization.* London and New York: Zed Books.

Zoomers, Annelies. 2003. "Land Liberalisation and Sustainable Development in Latin America: Unravelling the Land Sales Market of Santa Cruz, Bolivia." *International Development Planning Review,* 25, 3: 245–262.

1 The Soy Complex in Latin America

In 2003, Syngenta Corporation launched an advertising campaign with a map of a "United Soybean Republic" cutting across Argentina, Bolivia, Brazil, Paraguay and Uruguay with the slogan "the soybean knows no boundaries" (*la soya no conoce fronteras*). The image could not have been any clearer: transnational agribusiness was expanding its territorial control over Latin America. Indeed, from 2003 to 2005, Bolivia, Brazil, Paraguay and Uruguay legalized GM seed varieties, though the seeds were already being smuggled in from Argentina, which had legalized them in 1996 (Oliveira and Hecht 2016: 254). This officially marked the beginning of an economic and technological treadmill on which farmers became increasingly dependent on the technological packages associated with new high-yielding patented seeds, which, in turn, increased production costs. This chapter discusses the development of the soy complex in Latin America, from the commodification of the seed to the concentration of control over the upstream and downstream components of the value chain and its implications for agrarian change.

Commodification and Concentration Upstream

Following the legalization of GM varieties in Argentina, soybean plantations began to rapidly expand, from 17.5 million hectares in 1996 to 55.7 million in 2014 in the so-called "Soybean Republic," making the crop the most important in terms of both surface area and export value in the region (FAOSTAT 2016). Agricultural frontiers expanded into new and allegedly underutilized agro-ecological systems such as the Brazilian Cerrado, the Argentinian Pampas and Bolivia's eastern lowlands and led to widespread deforestation in important ecosystems such as the Amazon, the Atlantic Forest, the Gran Chaco and the Chiquitano forests, which cross territorial boundaries in the region (Hecht 2005; WWF 2014).

Figure 1.1 Hectares of Soybean Harvest in the "United Soybean Republic"

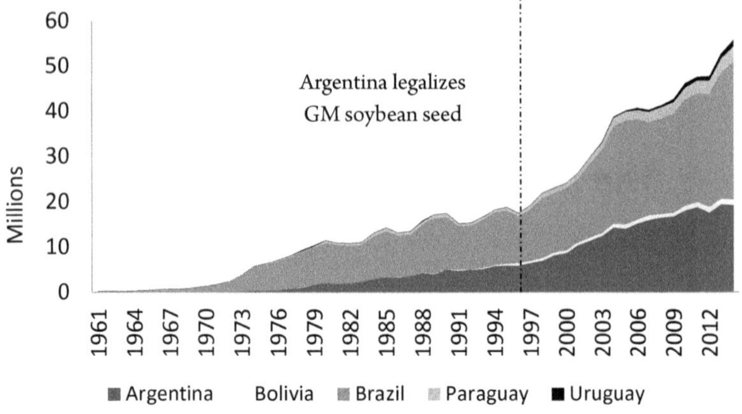

Source: FAOSTAT 2016.

The tropicalization and commercialization of GM soybean seeds was a success for the biotech industry, as soybeans were modified as a kind of "neo-nature" — "amenable to mechanized planting and harvesting, adapted to longer photoperiods and higher temperatures, and able to grow in more acidic, low-phosphorus soil conditions than the temperate areas of China, the USA and Ukraine" (Oliveira and Hecht 2016: 253). GM soybeans now account for 88 to 99 percent of total soybeans planted in the region and 83 percent globally (James 2015; WWF 2014). The GM seed, which is resistant to the herbicide glyphosate, enables farmers to use the herbicide in a no-tillage system in order to kill unwanted weeds that might affect the plant's growth. In theory, the use of glyphosate with glyphosate-resistant seeds is supposed to replace herbicides that are more toxic and thereby reduce herbicide volumes used in production (Cerdeira et al. 2011). However, studies by EMBRAPA, a state-owned research enterprise in Brazil, and Argentina's National Agricultural Technology Institute (Instituto Nacional de Tecnología Agropecuaria) have found that the persistent application of glyphosate in no-tillage monoculture production using GM seeds has led to the growing presence of various weed species resistant to the herbicide (Papa and Tuesca 2014; Cerdeira et al. 2011). This has led to not only a "direct link between the area of GM soybean and increases in the use of herbicides" but also a drastic increase in the volume and types of herbicides relative to the increase in the soybean-planted area (Catacora-Vargas et al. 2012: 30).

The combination of monocultures, overreliance on glyphosate due to the GM seed and neglect of other weed control measures has resulted in what the Union of Concerned Scientists call "the rise of superweeds" (USC 2013). Resistant to herbicides, these superweeds have infested some sixty million acres of US cropland and have led to the use of increased volumes of and more toxic herbicides and pesticides, contradicting the very logic of using GM seeds in the first place (USC 2013). This "pesticide treadmill" (Nicholls and Altieri 1997) has not only increased production costs for producers but also led to the greater application of agro-chemicals such as 2,4-D, atrazine and paraquat — the latter of which has been banned by the European Union due to high levels of toxicity and its implication in neurological and reproductive disorders (Catacora-Vargas et al. 2012). Yet, for companies such as Syngenta, which developed one of the most widely used paraquat-based herbicides, known as Gramoxone, the evolution of superweeds and the associated pesticide treadmill continue to increase their bottom line.

The industrial transformation of agriculture — first via mechanization, which reduced the need for labour, then through the dissemination of hybrid and GM seeds and finally through the dependence on agro-chemicals — has led to "a series of partial, discontinuous appropriations of the rural labour and biological production processes" (Goodman, Sorj and Wilkinson 1987: 2). This is what Goodman, Sorj and Wilkinson (1987: 3) refer to as "appropriationism," which is "constituted by the action of industrial capitals to reduce the importance of nature in rural production, and specifically as a force beyond their direction and control." With farmers increasingly dependent on GM seeds, agro-chemicals and machinery, industrial capital has penetrated agriculture by partially eliminating its material base and part of the natural production process incompatible with capital accumulation (Goodman, Sorj and Wilkinson 1987).

Not only has industry transformed agricultural production in its technical form, it has also changed the particular configurations of productive relations and forms of appropriation of the productive process. This has emerged through new forms of land and value-chain control, which exclude the rural majority and extract natural resources and appropriate rents and value from the production process. One of the principal forms of control has been through market concentration and consolidation of seed and chemical companies, which led to a market oligopoly largely controlled globally by the Big Six: Monsanto, Syngenta, Bayer, Dow Chemical, BASF and DuPont. By 2015, these companies controlled 75 percent of the global agro-chemical market, 63 percent of the commercial seed market and over 75 percent of private sector research in seeds and pesticides (ETC Group 2015). Moreover, just three companies (Syngenta, Bayer, BASF) controlled 49 percent of the global agro-chemicals market, while Monsanto, DuPont and Syngenta controlled 45 percent of the global seed market (ETC Group 2015). As recently as the 1970s, these markets were controlled by thousands of small-scale, mostly family-owned businesses (Howard 2015). The increased intellectual property protections for living organisms passed in the 1970s and 1980s, including full patent protections on transgenic seeds, attracted large firms, which rapidly acquired "hundreds of formerly independent biotechnology and seed companies" and eventually merged with each other to create the Big Six (Howard 2015: 2). Recently, the Big Six have undergone a new wave of mega-mergers, with Dow Chemical and DuPont merging into a new US$ 130 billion company, DowDuPont; ChemChina purchasing the Syngenta for US$ 43 billion, marking the largest Chinese overseas takeover in history; and Bayer taking over Monsanto for US$66 billion (Clapp 2018: 17). With BASF still a major player in the seed and agro-chemical global markets, the Big Six have turned into the Big Four.

The commodification of the seed — what Kloppenburg (2004: 37) calls the "biological nexus of farm-level production" — was the most important component for private industry's accumulation interests. Without both scientific innovation (research and development) and the introduction of new legislation, this would have never been possible. Since the seed reproduces itself as grain and can be replanted infinitely, legislation was required in order to separate the farmer from the reproduction of the seed — that is, from the agricultural means of production. Yet, as Newell and Glover (2003: 12) argue, not only does the biotech industry and the state share mutual interests for innovation and growth, "there is also evidence of a 'revolving door' between the biotechnology industry and government agencies." Mutual interests, "revolving door" politics, and powerful lobbyists from multinationals such as Monsanto are major reasons why such legislation gets passed.

As the seed became commodified and commercialized, so too did agricultural research. In the 1990s, private industry began to recruit leading scientific faculty and form strategic partnerships with public universities. In 1998, for example, Novartis (now Syngenta) signed a partnership with the University of California Berkeley's Department of Plant and Microbial Biology, which "gave Berkeley $25 million and access to Novartis' genomic database in return for a seat on departmental committees and first right to negotiate a license to patents from selected discoveries" (Kloppenburg 2004: 329). As transgenic crops became commercialized and more and more countries legalized GM varieties, the seed market became even more consolidated as the top ten seed firms acquired almost two hundred seed companies from 1996 to 2013 (Howard 2015). With the agro-chemical-seed market oligopoly, the Big Four now engage in cross-licensing agreements for transgenic seed traits — an effect "similar to the formation of a shared monopoly or cartel to exclude other potential competitors" (Howard 2015: 4). More than the material commodification and control of agro-inputs, the Big Four also control access to information and innovations. Their combined budget for agriculture research and development is some twenty times larger than that of the world's largest global agricultural innovation network CGIAR and fifteen times that of the United States Department of Agriculture's Agricultural Research Service budget for crop science research, giving them significant control over the agricultural research and development industry (ETC Group 2015). As Kloppenburg (2004: 10) argues, agricultural research has been "an important means of eliminating the barriers to the penetration of agriculture by capital" by commodifying agro-inputs and displacing productive activities off the farm and into an industrial setting. But while agricultural innovations are certainly important, it becomes problematic when a small, self-interested group dictates the research agenda and the interlinked technologies and products that are available in the market (see Miller and Conko 2001). With significant influence and control over the agricultural research agenda, the Big Four can invest in shaping agriculture's technical form through continued innovations that require their technological packages, complete with patented seeds, agro-chemical inputs and access to advanced mechanization. This control over information and knowledge production represents the power that agro-industry has over ideas, technological innovation and ultimately the terms of modern agricultural production.

Furthermore, just three farm equipment companies — Deere & Co. (John Deere), CNH (New Holland) and AGCO — combined for 49 percent of global farm equipment sales in 2013, some US$ 116 billion (ETC Group 2015). These equipment companies are collaborating with the Big Four in developing digital platforms such as Precision Planting and Climate FieldView, which give the industry complete control over every agricultural input decision from crop to seed variety to agro-chemicals (ETC Group 2015). This type of integration has enabled multinationals greater control over farmers, the production process and even the natural biological cycles of plant growth. It has also suppressed the value of farmer knowledge, as technological packages now dictate the terms and lengths of production. Institutional economists have suggested that "when four firms control 40 to 50 percent of a market, it is no longer competitive, as dominant firms can simply signal their intention to raise prices and the other will find it in their interest to follow suit" (Howard 2015: 3). This not only squeezes out the less capitalized competitors but creates a market oligopoly with a concentration of control and power. Industry has increasingly commodified and appropriated the upstream components of agricultural production — from machinery to fertilizers and seeds, and from agro-chemicals and biotechnologies to knowledge generation (research and development) — reducing the importance of nature in the rural production process via appropriationism (Goodman, Sorj and Wilkinson 1987). By doing so, the relative importance of the material base of agriculture has diminished, as industry can appropriate more surplus value from agro-industrial inputs and processing than from the actual agricultural production process itself. Even control over land becomes secondary if industry can control the upstream and downstream components of the market, forcing farmers to both purchase their value-added inputs and sell their final primary product to a market oligopoly. With such concentrated market power, the costs of these inputs — particularly seeds — have increased substantially, doubling in price per unit from 2005 to 2015 (USDA-ERS 2016).

Control and "Flexing" Downstream

Agro-industry's control does not stop at the upstream components of the market. Control over the downstream components — that is, everything after the crop is harvested, including storage, processing, packaging and distribution — is even more concentrated. The well-known ABCD (ADM, Bunge, Cargill, Louis Dreyfus) agribusiness firms control an estimated 75 to 90 percent of the global grain trade (Wesz Jr. 2016: 294). This type of oligopolistic market power obstructs competition and can lead to price fixing, as was the case in the 1990s when ADM was fined over US$ 100 million for colluding with other companies to raise prices for lysine and citric acid (Murphy, Burch and Clapp 2012).

In Latin America's Southern Cone, the ABCD firms began to gain prominence in the soy complex in the mid-1990s with the opening up to the global economy, the onset of neoliberal policies, the commercialization of GM varieties and the expansion of the region's agricultural frontiers. Primarily through mergers and acquisitions, the ABCD firms expanded their control over the region's soybeans from controlling 10 percent of the crushing capacity in 1995 to over 50 percent in 2011 (Wesz Jr. 2016: 294–295). Through vertical integration and, at times, collaboration with the Big Four, the ABCD firms have become integrated in various components of the production process such as technical assistance and the sale of inputs, financing and insurance schemes to farmers, as well as purchase, storage, processing, transportation and trade (Wesz Jr. 2016). Beyond vertical integration, the ABCD firms are increasingly expanding horizontally into complementary markets such as energy, industrial material and finance.

The multiple and flexible uses of agro-industrial crops for feed, food, fuel and industrial materials have also facilitated the integration of these firms into different sectors (Borras et al. 2016). With just 6 percent of the world's soybean crop used directly as human food without industrial processing, soybeans have become the quintessential agro-industrial flex crop (Oliveira and Schneider 2016). Approximately 85 percent of world production is processed into meal and oil, with 98 percent of the meal used for animal feed and 95 percent of the oil component used as edible oil (Soyatech 2016). The remainder of the meal is further processed as soy flour and protein, while the rest of the oil is used as an industrial input for products such as soaps, biodiesel and fatty acids, among many others (Soyatech 2016; Oliveira and Schneider 2016).

The industrialization of agriculture has been further intensified through the financialization of land and agriculture as both new and old actors increasingly engage in speculation and hedging. Following the financial crisis of 2007–08 and subsequent food price hike in 2008, investors started to target farmland as a secure investment alternative since it is strongly correlated with inflation and is thus "touted as an inflation hedge and an excellent way to reduce portfolio risk through diversification" (Fairbairn 2014: 778). Though farmland increasingly is turned into a financial asset for hedgers and speculators, as well as within agribusiness, it also retains its productive capacity as a use value. This "dual nature" of farmland, as Fairbairn (2014: 786) points out, makes it possible "to use the land productively while simultaneously speculating on financial returns from its appreciation." The financialization of agriculture, including the financial service divisions of the ABCDs, has intricately linked finance, food and agriculture due to financial deregulation and the new types of derivatives that often bundle a variety of non-food and agricultural commodities, enabling investors to significantly influence both food and land prices (Murphy, Burch and Clapp 2012). This has not only reinforced unequal relations of power among farmers, agribusiness and new financial actors far removed from production but has also led to increasing food price volatility on international markets (Isakson 2014).

As the upstream and downstream components of agriculture become increasingly controlled by a few multinational corporations and capital continues its penetration of agriculture through appropriationism, flexing and financialization, important implications arise for rural populations —

especially small-scale, capital-poor farmers — and the environment. Agro-industry integrates farmers into their value chains, requiring the purchase and use of certain seeds and chemical inputs (upstream) in order to comply with standardized market requirements (downstream) controlled by the same agro-industrial market oligopoly. These new institutional arrangements bind farmers into cycles of debt and dependency, altering their relationship and access to land and other factors of production in subtler ways than physical dispossession or displacement. Rather than becoming fully proletarianized, there is a tendency for farmers to progressively enter into contradictory class positions — between labour and capital — effectively impeding their ability to organize as a class for itself and apply pressure from below to improve their socioeconomic position in society.

(Trans-)Latin American Capital, Pools de Siembra and Contract Farming

Although the ABCD firms did expand their control over the soybean complex in the Southern Cone, the influence of regional actors in the soy complex cannot be discounted. Many Brazilian and Argentinian large-scale landowners and entrepreneurs have developed *pools de siembra* (sowing pools), whereby farm management companies pool resources to increase bargaining power and to achieve economies of scale through input purchases, access to storage and processing facilities. This enabled Brazilian and Argentinian agribusiness firms such as Cresud-BrasilAgro, Amaggi–Bom Futuro, Adecoagro, SLC Agricola, El Tejar, TIAA-CREF Global Agriculture, V-Agro, MSU and Los Grobo to expand through the Southern Cone and establish themselves as major players among the ABCD firms (Oliveira and Hecht 2016). Of particular significance are two of region's largest landowners, Blairo Maggi, owner of Amaggi–Bom Futuro of Brazil, and Gustavo Grobocopatel, owner of Los Grobo of Argentina. These agricultural entrepreneurs have been pioneers of the soybean complex in the region, developing and expanding their enterprises both upstream and downstream alongside the ABCD firms. Amaggi–Bom Futuro also engages in strategic joint ventures with Bunge and Louis Dreyfus (Oliveira and Hecht 2016: 261–264). The so-called foreignization involving Brazilian agro-capitalists expanding their control over the region is about the changing forms and relations of production rather than the fact that they are foreign or Brazilian. It is the expansion of capital into "undercapitalized" frontiers, or new greenfield sites where more surplus value can be extracted and appropriated. The agro-industrial soy complex has introduced a variety of institutional arrangements that enable some actors to derive benefits from both natural (land-based resources) and productive (capital, technology, labour) resources while excluding others, regardless of land ownership. These include arrangements such as contract farming (Wesz Jr. 2016), small-scale land leasing or the *partida* arrangement, where one party supplies the land and the other the equipment and inputs (McKay and Colque 2016), *pools de siembra* (Craviotti 2016) and combinations of these between and among farmers and agro-industry.

Pools de siembra represent new contractual arrangements that combine land, capital and human resources across scales, levels and actors. The model originated in Argentina in the late 1980s with the Alvarado family (El Tejar) and the Grobocopatel family (Los Grobo), who own and lease some 1.4 million hectares and 420,000 hectares, respectively, across the Southern Cone (Oliveira and Hecht 2016: 262–264). *Pools de siembra* can refer to a variety of "innovative arrangements" including "leasing or providing property in trust, contracting machines and services, using technology packages based on modern machinery, heavily utilising biotechnology or agrochemicals and incorporating digital systems and individuals who specialise in field selection, production, management and marketing" (Murmis and Murmis 2012: 491). The increased financialization of land and agriculture and the convergence of sectors as they become more integrated in agro-industrial value chains have rendered *pools de siembra* much more complex, involving a variety of investors far removed from the production process. In Argentina, Murmis and Murmis (2012: 501) find that the expansion of *pools de siembra* tends to lead to land concentration as large farms gradually displace smaller farms. Given that economies of scale have increased in importance with the development of agro-industry's capital-intensive forms of production, market mechanisms favour larger-scale production, pressuring smaller-scale producers to sell or lease their land.

While *pools de siembra* have also taken root in Paraguay and Uruguay, individual leases and purchases are much more common. Land concentration occurs through the amalgamation of successive purchases in a given area, indebtedness of capital-poor farmers (due to the intensive capital requirements of soybean production) who are forced to sell their land and forcible displacement through violence or soil contamination (Galeano 2012; Ezquerro-Cañete 2016; Elgert 2015). In Paraguay, Brazilian capital has come to dominate soybean production, originating with cross-border migrations in the 1970s, and consolidating more recently with agribusiness expansion (Galeano 2012). According to Galeano (2012: 463), "Brazilians rank first both in terms of the amount of land they own and in terms of the number of regions where they have invested in recent years (2006–2010)," while Wesz (2016: 289) finds that "90 percent of Paraguayan soy is produced by Brazilians or their descendants." In Uruguay, land leasing and purchases have also increased substantially in recent years. From 2000 to 2010, 39 percent of the country's agricultural area (roughly 6.4 million hectares) was purchased, while another 45 percent (roughly 7.3 million hectares) was leased, mostly by multinational companies and investment funds, as well as Argentinian, Brazilian and domestic companies (Piñeiro 2012: 483–485). Piñeiro (2012: 484) explains how a combination of purchasing and leasing is becoming more common, particularly among Argentinian companies, by "buying a tract of land; establishing a base of operations and machinery on that land; and leasing surrounding lands on which to expand production. This strategy reduces the capital investment in land, but ensures control of a large area."

Most common among those who actually put land into production is contract farming, especially among the more well-off medium- and large-scale landholders who own agricultural machinery such as tractors and harvesters. These capital-rich farmers tend to lease the land of others or rent out their services (sowing, fumigating, harvesting) to capital-poor farmers. Many of these farmers are part of associations, whereby the association pools their resources together in order to achieve economies of scale and negotiate with input suppliers, processors and traders — a kind of small-scale, cooperative-based *pool de siembra*. Indeed, even the large-scale *pools de siembra* are a form of contract farming among investors, various farmers and agribusiness firms.

As agro-industry expands its control over the upstream and downstream components of production, their power to control, regulate and dictate the terms of production also increases. As Wesz (2016: 298) puts it, "The more firm dependent producers become, the less farmer friendly contracts established with the companies will be, involving differences in interests rates, input prices, deadlines for delivery of goods, and the general conditions of the contracts."

Proponents of contract farming, such as the World Bank, suggest that contract farmers "have significantly higher incomes than other farmers" and that "producer organizations and contract farming are essential for these smallholders to take part in value chains and cater to supermarket demands" (World Bank 2007: 127, 241). This argument is based on the need to integrate farmers with markets and is once again based on a residual logic and technical approach, neglecting important relational aspects of power and access. It rests on a neo-institutional framework focusing on transaction costs, economies of scale, efficiency, coordination failures and access to technology, among other factors. But what fails to be taken into account are the power relations between participants, the sociopolitical environments in which implementation takes place, the types of farmers who are likely to benefit or not and those who will be excluded and how it will affect farmer differentiation (White 1997; Oya 2012).

While there is great diversity of contract farming schemes, farmers ultimately become incorporated into broader circuits of capital accumulation, shift their cultivation from diversified domestic crop production to export-oriented monocultures and become much more dependent on the dictates of international (agro)commodity prices and external industrial inputs while entering into cycles of debt and dependency (White 1997; McMichael 2013). In effect, agro-industrial capital is able to extend its territorial reach without owning the land; assuming risks such as price fluctuations, natural disasters and crop failures; or facing threats of expropriation from above or below. Contract farming thus represents a form of control without dispossession, which nonetheless produces farmer differentiation, exclusion and marginalization.

Conclusion

Technological innovation has enabled the persistent penetration of industrial and financial capital into agriculture. Fuelled by neo-Malthusian logics and theories of modernization, achieving maximum yields and expanding agricultural frontiers into otherwise unsuitable soils has become the model for agricultural development. The agro-food sector has become increasingly corporatized and concentrated, largely controlled by a few multinational firms that collaborate among themselves to control the upstream and downstream components of the agro-industrial complex. Green Revolution technologies developed in the Cerrado region, such as new hybrid and GM seeds, agro-chemical inputs and capital-intensive mechanized production, expanded outwards from the south of Brazil. Appropriationism, substitutionism, flexing and financialization characterized this process, as new agrarian relations and forms of control emerged in the countryside. *Pools de siembra* and various types of contract farming have enabled industrial and financial capital to control and appropriate value from agricultural production without necessarily owning the land. This has and continues to incorporate classes of rural labour into industrial value chains, mostly in adverse ways. This chapter has examined how, where and to what extent agro-industry developed in Latin America, the forms it has taken and some of the implications for agrarian change.

The following chapters delve more deeply into these dynamics in Bolivia, situating the country's agrarian structure in historical context, the development of the soy complex and the new mechanisms of control, exclusion and extraction that have emerged.

REFERENCES

Borras, Saturnino M. Jr., Jennifer C. Franco, S. Ryan Isakson, Les Levidow, and Pietje Vervest. 2016. "The Rise of Flex Crops and Commodities: Implications for Research." *Journal of Peasant Studies,* 43, 1: 93–115.

Catacora-Vargas, Georgina, Pablo Galeano, Sarah Zanon Agapito-Tenfen, Darìo Aranda, Tomàs Palau, and Rubens Onofre Nodari. 2012. *Soybean Production in the Southern Cone of the Americas: Update on Land and Pesticide Use.* <genok.com/wp-content/uploads//2013/03/Soybean-Production-in-the-Southern-Cone-of-the-Americas-Update-on-Land-and-Pesticide-Use.pdf>

Cerdeira, Antonio L., Dionsio LP Gazziero, Stephen O. Duke, and Marcus B. Matallo. 2011. "Agricultural Impacts of Glyphosate-Resistant Soybean Cultivation in South America." *Journal of Agricultural and Food Chemistry,* 59, 11: 5799–5807.

Clapp, Jennifer. 2018. "Mega-Mergers on the Menu: Corporate Concentration and the Politics of Sustainability in the Global Food System." *Global Environmental Politics,* 18, 2: 12–33.

Craviotti, Clara. 2016. "Which Territorial Embeddedness? Territorial Relationships of Recently Internationalized Firms of the Soybean Chain." *Journal of Peasant Studies,* 43, 2: 331–347.

Elgert, Laureen. 2015. "'More Soy on Fewer Farms' in Paraguay: Challenging Neoliberal Agriculture's Claims to Sustainability." *Journal of Peasant Studies,* 43, 2: 537–561.

ETC Group. 2015. *Breaking Bad: Big Ag Mega-Mergers in Play Dow + DuPont in the Pocket? Next: Demonsanto?* Ottawa: ETC Group.

Ezquerro-Cañete, Arturo. 2016. "Poisoned, Dispossessed and Excluded: A Critique of the Neoliberal Soy Regime in Paraguay." *Journal of Agrarian Change,* 16, 4: 702–710.

Fairbairn, Madeleine. 2014. "'Like Gold with Yield': Evolving Intersections between Farmland and Finance." *Journal of Peasant Studies,* 41, 5: 777–795.

FAOSTAT (Food and Agriculture Organization). 2016. "Food Balance." Rome.

Galeano, Luis A. 2012. "Paraguay and the Expansion of Brazilian and Argentinian Agribusiness Frontiers." *Canadian Journal of Development Studies / Revue Canadienne d ' Études Du Développement,* 33, 4: 458–470.

Goodman, David, Bernardo Sorj, and John Wilkinson. 1987. *From Farming to Biotechnology: A Theory of Agro-Industrial Development.* Oxford, UK: Basil Blackwell.

Hecht, Susanna B. 2005. "Soybeans, Development and Conservation on the Amazon Frontier." *Development and Change,* 36, 2: 375–404.

Howard, Philip H. 2015. "Intellectual Property and Consolidation in the Seed Industry." *Crop Science,* 55, 6: 1–7.

Isakson, S. Ryan. 2014. "Food and Finance: The Financial Transformation of Agro-Food Supply Chains." *Journal of Peasant Studies,* 41, 5: 749–775.
James, Clive. 2015. *20th Anniversary (1996 to 2015) of the Global Commercialization of Biotech Crops and Biotech Crop Highlights in 2015*. Ithaca, NY: ISAAA.
Kloppenburg, Jack Ralph. 2004. *First the Seed: The Political Economy of Plant Biotechnology*. Second. Madison, Wisconsin: The University of Wisconsin Press.
McKay, Ben, and Gonzalo Colque. 2016. "Bolivia's Soy Complex: The Development of 'Productive Exclusion.'" *Journal of Peasant Studies,* 43, 2: 583–610.
McMichael, Philip. 2013. "Value-Chain Agriculture and Debt Relations: Contradictory Outcomes." *Third World Quarterly,* 34, 4: 671–690.
Miller, H.I., and G. Conko. 2001. "Precaution without Principle." *Nature Biotechnology,* 19, 4: 302–303.
Murmis, Miguel, and Maria R. Murmis. 2012. "Land Concentration and Foreign Land Ownership in Argentina in the Context of Global Land Grabbing." *Canadian Journal of Development Studies/Revue Canadienne d'études Du Développement,* 33, 4: 417–438.
Murphy, Sophia, David Burch, and Jennifer Clapp. 2012. *Cereal Secrets: The World's Largest Commodity Traders and Global Trends in Agriculture. Oxfam Research Report*. Oxford: Oxfam International.
Newell, Peter, and Dominic Glover. 2003. *Business and Biotechnology: Regulation and the Politics of Influence,* 192. *IDS Working Paper*. Brighton.
Nicholls, Clara I., and Miguel A. Altieri. 1997. "Conventional Agricultural Development Models and the Persistence of the Pesticide Treadmill in Latin America." *International Journal of Sustainable Development and World Ecology,* 4: 93–111.
Oliveira, Gustavo de L.T., and Susanna Hecht. 2016. "Sacred Groves, Sacrifice Zones and Soy Production: Globalization, Intensification and Neo-Nature in South America." *Journal of Peasant Studies,* 43, 2: 251–285.
Oliveira, Gustavo de L.T., and Mindi Schneider. 2016. "The Politics of Flexing Soybeans: China, Brazil and Global Agroindustrial Restructuring." *Journal of Peasant Studies,* 43, 1: 167–194.
Oya, Carlos. 2012. "Contract Farming in Sub-Saharan Africa A Survey of Approaches, Debates and Issues." *Journal of Agrarian Change,* 12, 1: 1–33.
Papa, J.C., and D. Tuesca. 2014. *Los Problemas Actuales de Malezas En La Región Sojera Núcleo Argentina: Origen y Alternativas de Manejo*. Buenos Aires.
Pederson, Palle. 2007. "Soybean Uses." Iowa State University — Soybean Extension and Research Program.
Piñeiro, Diego E. 2012. "Land Grabbing: Concentration and 'Foreignisation' of Land in Uruguay." *Canadian Journal of Development Studies/Revue Canadienne d'Études Du Développement,* 33, 4: 471–489.
Soyatech. 2016. "Soy Facts." St. Louis, MO: United States Soybean Board/US Soybean Export Council.
USC (Union of Concerned Scientists). 2013. *The Rise of Superweeds — and What to Do About It*. Cambride.
USDA-ERS (United States Department of Agriculture Economic Research Services). 2016. "Commodity Costs and Returns." Washington.

Wesz Jr, Valdemar João. 2016. "Strategies and Hybrid Dynamics of Soy Transnational Companies in the Southern Cone." *Journal of Peasant Studies*, 43, 2: 286–312.

White, Ben. 1997. "Agroindustry and Contract Farmers in Upland West Java." *Journal of Peasant Studies*, 24, 3: 100–136.

World Bank. 2007. *World Development Report 2008: Agriculture for Development. World Development Report 2008*. Washington.

WWF (World Wildlilfe Fund). 2014. *The Growth of Soy Impacts and Solutions*. Gland, Switzerland.

2 Land Control: Bolivia's Agrarian Structure and Frontier Expansion

> Soy is a business for big producers; the smaller ones cannot survive without government support. With the current government's policies, there is no future for small producers, they will eventually have to sell and move to the cities.
>
> — *Iglenio Klaus, large-scale landowner*

Bolivia's contemporary agrarian structure developed through various phases of the country's development and transition — from independence in 1825, the revolution in 1952, through to the neoliberal reforms of 1985 to 2005. This chapter traces this development and reveals the influence of Cold War politics and US geopolitical interests through the use of Public Law 480 and the Bohan Plan's "march to the east" in shaping Bolivia's present-day agrarian structure.[1] In the mid-1980s public policies started encouraging foreign investment, the economy (and the agricultural sector) became deregulated and frontier expansion was prioritized with an agro-industrial bias. Soybean production started to develop, though it did not take off until the 1990s — much later than its neighbouring Southern Cone countries, particularly Brazil and Argentina. This chapter presents an overview of the development and expansion of the agricultural frontier, the politics behind these processes and the shifting relations between state, societal and capitalist actors before the rise of Evo Morales and MAS to state power.

Historical Context

Bolivia gained its independence from the Spanish in 1825, but the vast majority of Bolivians remained marginalized, excluded from political participation and subordinated to a landed elite and conservative oligarchy until the mid-twentieth century. From independence to the 1950s, approximately 2 percent of the total population voted in elections, as Indigenous Peoples were excluded from voting, and only 2 to 3 percent of the country's total available agricultural land was under cultivation, nearly all of which was located in the mountainous altiplano region near La Paz and its nearby valleys (Malloy 1970). This was largely due to the location of Indigenous communities (labourers) who had settled and remained concentrated in the altiplano since the pre-Inca period. Since labour was the main input for production, agricultural expansion remained limited to where exploitable labour was available and thus concentrated in the altiplano, leaving the vast majority of the country's most fertile land underutilized, particularly in the lowlands of Santa Cruz. The hacienda (large-scale landed estates) regime expropriated the lands of Indigenous communities, often allowing Indigenous families usufruct rights to a small parcel on the hacienda so long as they worked as labourers for the *hacendado* (estate owner) (Kay and Urioste 2007).

Civil wars and internal tensions came to a peak in 1952, when the military and oligarchs were confronted by the MNR, which had garnered support among miners, peasants, national police and the powerful Bolivian Workers' Confederation (Central Obrera Boliviana) (Grindle 2000). As conflict spread quickly throughout the country, the military disintegrated, as armed peasant, miner, Indigenous and other wage labourers aligned to drive landed elites and mine owners off their land. Many Indigenous Peoples (referred to as "*indios*" at the time) began to self-identify as peasants (*campesinos*) and a national trade union was formed uniting Quechas, Aymaras and other peasants in the National Confederation of Peasant Workers of Bolivia (Confederación Nacional de Trabajadores Campesinos de Bolivia)[2] which was closely linked to the MNR government (Albó 2002). The MNR took state power in 1952, and began implementing important reforms including universal adult suffrage, which allowed Indigenous people to vote, the nationalization of the majority of the mining industry and the redistribution of some 30 percent of the country's agricultural land to over 200,000 rural families (Grindle 2000; Klein 2011). Prior to the agrarian reform, Bolivia had one of the most unequal agrarian structures in Latin America, whereby just 6 percent of landowners controlled 92 percent of the land, with the average estate over one thousand hectares using just 1.5 percent of the land (Klein 2011). With the country's best lands underutilized, Bolivia was dependent on food imports to feed its population. Since many of the landed elites were absentee landowners with little capital invested, peasant mobilization and redistribution by expropriation were not heavily contested.

By the mid-1950s, however, annual inflation rates surged to over 900 percent, drastically devaluing the currency and triggering a financial crisis (Klein 2011). The fiscal crisis threatened the MNR's ability to govern, as social and economic upheavals were on the rise. With the Cold War in full swing, US president Dwight D. Eisenhower was wary of the emergence of revolutionary regimes hostile to US interests springing up throughout the region. The US quickly offered financial and food aid under Public Law 480, and by the late 1950s Bolivia was "the largest single recipient of United States foreign aid in Latin America and the highest per capita in the world" (Klein 2011: 218). Initially, food aid was necessary to alleviate hunger, but the persistent dumping of US subsidized milled wheat flooded the Bolivian market and undermined the development of Bolivia's own wheat sector, for both peasants and millers.

A two-track agricultural development strategy was designed by US government officials and funded through a $25-million agreement with the US Export–Import Bank to promote economic development (Thorn 1971). Led by US State Department official Merwin L. Bohan, the "Bohan Plan" "recommended that the population be shifted from the poor lands of the altiplano to the fertile lands of the east" (Thorn 1971: 165). The ensuing migration, referred to as the "march to the east" (*marcha al oriente*), offered highland peasants 20 to 50 hectares of land in San Julián, Cuatro Cañadas and the surrounding region in the lowlands of Santa Cruz to produce traditional crops for domestic consumption while also providing large-scale farms with an abundant supply of labour. By 1980, 41 percent of the population of Santa Cruz were highlanders. Large-scale parcels, referred to as enterprises not latifundium,[3] were also distributed to capitalist entrepreneurs and political elites, who received landholdings of 500 to 50,000 hectares (Valdivia 2010).

By 1985, hyperinflation and a debt crisis led to the adoption of the Jeffrey Sachs–inspired[4] New Economic Plan with swift cuts in government spending (including subsidies on food and public services), wage freezes and reduced public sector employment, tax system reform, liberalized trade, currency devaluation and new international agreements "to allow foreign guarantees for foreign investors" (Van Dijck 1998: 32). The combined lack of state subsidies and support services, trade liberalization and the designation of peasant production to an "economically marginal" (Sanabria 1999: 539) role resulted in a rural poverty rate of nearly 90 percent in the lowlands of Santa Cruz in 1994 (Vos, Haeduck and Mejia 1998). The urban-rural income gap widened and the terms of trade in agriculture declined as peasant farming remained stagnant and industrial crops for export were prioritized (Vos, Haeduck and Mejia 1998). Traditional crops from the Andean region such as traditional maize varieties, potato, onion, wheat, quinoa, broad bean and alfalfa suffered a negative 7 percent growth rate from 1991 to 1997, while industrial crops (maize, wheat, rice, sugarcane, cotton, soybean, sunflower and sorghum) in Santa Cruz destined mainly for export grew 124 percent during the same period (Kay and Urioste 2007).

In 1991, the World Bank's Eastern Lowland Project was implemented to expand the production of agricultural commodities, particularly soybeans, with the aim of increasing exports to 200,000 tons per year and domestically producing 30,000 tons of wheat per year to replace imported wheat after the sector had been virtually destroyed by imports under Public Law 480 (World Bank 1998). This project was explicitly oriented to consolidate large-scale industrial crop production under the rationale that it would accelerate economic growth and lead to sustainable agricultural development. As such a "landlord bias" became evident, whereby "public policy discriminates against rural workers and poor peasants in favour of landlords and rural capitalists" (Kay 2009: 112). Investment and frontier expansion during this period represent an important transition in the forms and relations that characterized agricultural production at the time.

This period entailed a rapid incorporation of frontier land into soybean plantations as the form of production began to shift from labour-intensive to extensive mechanization, driving deforestation (Barber et al. 1996; Müller et al. 2013). Other crops such as sugarcane and cotton remained slow-growing commodities. Highland peasants and Mennonite settlers also began to expand cultivated areas to increase rice, maize and wheat production for the internal market. While large properties began to adopt capital-intensive farming, smallholders still had the advantage of controlling labour-intensive farming, maintaining their productive capacity and their access to land and (family) labour. Peasant agriculture in the altiplano, however, suffered immensely as the state's structural adjustment program's "landlord bias" focused on developing the agro-industrial export sector in the east. As Kay and Urioste (2007: 53) point out, "Up until the policies of structural adjustment of 1985, the internal (food) supply was able to meet the demand of the Bolivian population but, with the ability to freely import foodstuffs from 1985, the peasant economy declined as it could not compete with the better quality and cheaper imports." The subsequent stagnation of agricultural production in the western altiplano coincided with rapid increases in the eastern lowlands — in terms of cultivated land, productivity and migration, as even more highland peasants went east in search of land or labour opportunities. This provided large-scale farmers with a stable supply of rural wage labour, even though labour requirements for production were gradually decreasing.

During the period of neoliberal social reformism (Assies 2000) or what Charles Hale (2002: 487) refers to as neoliberal multiculturalism, "whereby proponents of the neoliberal doctrine pro-actively endorse a substantive, if limited, version of indigenous cultural rights, as a means to resolve their own problems and advance their own political agendas," the second agrarian reform (Law 1715 of 1996) was passed. One of the key objectives of the reform was to formalize property rights (*saneamiento*) as a form of state-building in order to "make society legible" (Scott 1998). By doing so, the state could generate tax revenues from agricultural lands and thus stimulate production by making sure lands did not sit idle for speculative accumulation and thus fulfilled a socioeconomic legal function (*Función Económica y Social*) (Albó 2002). Indigenous territories (Tierra Comunitaria de Orígen, TCO) and small farms were also prioritized with new legal protections and tax exemptions. Law 1715 aimed to recover illegal landholdings to redistribute to peasant and Indigenous communities. This initiative pursued legitimate principles of social justice for the peasant and Indigenous majority. However, economically and politically powerful groups launched an open confrontation with the intention of neutralizing this initiative by the state to expand its control over the lowlands of Santa Cruz. The legal struggle became a political struggle (Valdivia 2010).

The implementation of the new land law meant that all fallow lands should have reverted to the state. However, large-scale landowners represented by the National Agricultural Confederation (Confederación Nacional de Agricultura) reinforced their demands for the protection of private property and fought against any redistribution of pre-existing property (Urioste 2007). This sectorial political resistance, with heavy economic and political clout in Santa Cruz, was extremely effective, as the land titling process produced marginal results — less than 10 percent of land targeted by titling was actually titled — by the end of 2004. As Valdivia (2010) explains, the Santa Cruz elite formed a regional hegemony built on legitimation narratives representing themselves as successful producers and proclaiming that small-scale producers and peasants, too, could become successful capitalist agricultural entrepreneurs. In addition to the political resistance of agribusiness, another factor that led to the land law's ineffectiveness in redistribution was that the unproductive lands of the early 1990s became controlled by capitalist farmers from Brazil, Argentina and Bolivia who bought huge tracts of land and expanded their landholdings. This hampered the reversal of large and medium-sized properties since previously idle land was now being put into production, allowing owners to meet all requirements to protect their private property. The land reform was left largely "unfinished," with an estimated 100,000 families left landless, and the persistence of rural poverty as a "landlord bias" in the eastern lowlands continued to marginalize peasants, small-scale farmers and rural wage labourers — and most severely Indigenous people and women (Kay 2009; Kay and Urioste 2007).

Foreign Capital and Soybean Expansion

The 1990s was a decade with visible incursions of foreign capital, not only in the soybean sector but also towards acquiring cattle ranches in remote areas of the frontier. In just fifteen years (1985–2000), the area under soybean cultivation in Bolivia increased from 50,000 hectares to 500,000 hectares (ANAPO 2015). The rapid expansion of the agricultural frontier over a relatively short time period was carried out with little regulatory oversight regarding legal land tenure. The land market was "open for business," as Iglenio Klaus, a Brazilian farmer working in Bolivia, explained to me. In the 1990s, the Bolivian government was so eager to attract investment that land was almost given away for free. Farmers were buying land in what is now called the soybean expansion zone for $20–$30 per hectare. In 2014–15, those same lands sold for $2,000 to $5,000 per hectare. Formal and informal land transactions were widespread, as Bolivia's land market was a magnet for capitalized farmers given rising production costs in neighbouring countries.

Klaus, for example, is a large-scale landowner from Rio Grande do Sul, Brazil. He grew up in Brazil's southern-most state during the initial soy boom triggered by trade relations with Japan in the 1970s. As land prices increased dramatically in his home state, he saw Bolivia as an opportunity to expand his landholdings and continue farming with much lower costs of production. He arrived to San Julián in 1990 and purchased 1,400 hectares of land for US$30 per hectare, half of which he now uses for soybean production and half for cattle pasture. At the time, there was virtually no mechanized agriculture, as labour-intensive production prevailed. Klaus brought his machinery from Brazil, as did many others during the 1990s. He explained that he could now sell his land for at least US$3000 per hectare but similar land just across the Brazilian border in the state of Mato Grosso would cost US$20,000 to $30,000 per hectare. Furthermore, production costs are much lower in Bolivia because diesel is subsidized by the state, making it approximately 30 percent of the cost in Brazil. "Not only is Brazil's land more expensive, along with the cost of inputs," explained Klaus, but "it is also harder to maintain fertility. The quality of land in Bolivia (in this region) is much better because it is younger." Since the majority of the Bolivian lowlands were native forests only a decade before, the soil fertility has likely not reached the point of exhaustion and salinity from agro-chemical inputs that land in Brazil has from undergoing monoculture production for much longer.

When asked about the Bolivian government, Klaus was relatively satisfied. "The government has been good for producers and the economy in general, prices and exchange rates have been stable, private property is more secure and you can work your land in peace," he said. But while such laws are favourable for large-scale producers and landowners, Klaus explained that smaller farmers suffer. "Soy is a business for big producers," he explained. "The smaller ones cannot survive without government support. With the current government's policies, there is no future for small producers. They will eventually have to sell and move to the cities." While there can be a tendency to villainize foreign large-scale capitalist farmers, Klaus was critical of the state for not supporting smallholders. He thought the state needed to invest in what he called "agro-villages," which could work as cooperatives, sharing farm equipment and building strong farmer-to-farmer networks, but which would require technical assistance and rural infrastructure. He was also critical of the land concentration in general, revealing that loopholes in the land ceiling of 5,000 hectares allowed people to simply register properties under different family member names. His Brazilian friend owns 50 properties, but none of them are in his name, so he is able to control some 20,000 hectares without any problems. In this way, Klaus said, the system works for the interests of large-scale farmers but against those of smallholders. Despite living in Bolivia for over 20 years, Klaus still did not feel part of Bolivia or his community. His wife is Bolivian, but he feels Bolivians discriminate against him because of the land he owns and the fact that he is a foreigner.

Another Brazilian producer, Claudio Batista Vega from Paraná, went to Bolivia in 1996 to take advantage of the much cheaper and available land. Batista owns 430 hectares, works another 270 hectares for farmers with no machinery and recently bought two properties from his neighbours (40 hectares each) at a price of US$1,200 per hectare. He also owns land in

Brazil, but he left that for his children to work as he went across the border to expand production. He continues to travel between Bolivia and Brazil based on sowing and harvest cycles, living in both countries throughout the year. Batista explained that he had purchased his 430 hectares for US$50 per hectare and could sell the lot for US$6,000 per hectare since it is top-quality fertile land producing 3.5 tons of soybean per hectare, which is almost double the region's average. Similar to Klaus, Batista did not feel part of the Bolivian community and felt discriminated against for being a foreign landowner. However, he has never had any problems with the Bolivian state and works his land in peace, which, for him, is all that he needs. When asked about the possibility to expand his landholdings, Batista said, "There is no opportunity to expand. Though the government says there is land, it is poor quality. All the good land in Bolivia worth working is already taken."

These two portraits of Brazilians working the land in Bolivia are exemplary of the changing relations of access and control over land prompted by the development of the soy complex and new capitalist actors. These are the middle- and large-scale landowners from Brazil, Argentina and Bolivia who engage in contract farming schemes with agribusinesses such as Cargill, ADM, Gravetal, FINO and so on, where they purchase seeds and agro-chemical inputs and establish forward contracts that establish the price paid at harvest based on the Chicago Board of Trade. These capitalized farmers with tractors and harvesters are the minority in the region, representing just 6 percent of total producers in San Julián and 17 percent in Cuatro Cañadas (INE 2015). These farmers are incorporating and absorbing the lands of undercapitalized farmers either through various contract arrangements, usually referred to as the *partida* arrangement, and through outright land purchases, as explained by Batista, who bought the adjacent parcels of his neighbours. These processes, referred to as productive exclusion, are discussed in more detail in the next chapter.

The Emergence of a New Social Movement

The agrarian dynamics described above coincided with important struggles in urban areas. Severe inequalities, particularly between classes of capital and labour but also between urban and rural, men and women, non-Indigenous and Indigenous, were accentuated when Bolivian president Hugo Banzer (1997–2001), in collusion with foreign capital, privatized Cochabamba's water supply company, Municipal Drinking Water and Sewage Service (Servicio Municipal de Agua Potable y Alcantarillado), which drastically increased water tariffs. The fifteen years of neoliberal reforms, which cut public spending, privatized public services, deregulated the economy and liberalized trade, culminated during Cochabamba's Water War when an unprecedented alliance among various class fractions of labour, including the Federation of Irrigators' Organizations of Cochabamba (Federación Departamental Cochabambina de Regantes), the Federation of Factory Workers of Cochabamba (Federación Departamental de Trabajadores Fabriles de Cochabamba), neighbourhood associations, potable-water committees, the Unified Confederation of Peasants of Bolivia, Indigenous groups and others concerned about their rising water bills — all united under the representation of the Coordination for the Defence of Water and Life (Coordinadora por la Defensa del Agua y la Vida), a network-based structure linking together different types of organizations (Assies, 2003). They united against not only the privatization of the water supply but also the neoliberal reforms that had led to their continued exclusion and marginalization since 1985 (Assies 2003). The clear state-capital alliance had become evident to classes of labour, leading to a legitimacy crisis of the state as class alliances from the urban to the rural and across sectors converged in protest. It was a unique moment in which an alliance formed among such diverse urban and rural workers, peasants, NGOs and others in the community.

This movement was accompanied with intellectual support from the Commune group (grupo Comuna), led by leading Marxist-oriented scholars such as Luis Tapia, Raúl Prada, Raquel Gutiérrez Aguilar and future vice president Álvaro García Linera, among others — whom we might refer to as organic intellectuals representing the interests of the excluded, marginalized and exploited classes (Gramsci 1971). The group published a series of works beginning in 1999 criticizing neoliberal capitalism's assault on Bolivian society over the previous fifteen years and more broadly throughout the Latin American region. Their work revived Bolivian Marxist scholarship with an ethnic dimension located within class analyses and inspired by the works of renowned Bolivian sociologist René Zavaleta Mercado, particularly his concept of Bolivia as a motley society (*sociedad abigarrada*) representing the complexity of Bolivia's ethnic and class dimensions (Zavaleta Mercado 1986). Indeed, Gutiérrez Aguilar and García Linera were part of the earlier Katarista movement, which had facilitated a coalition of Indigenous, peasant and worker movements in the 1970s. Members of the Comuna were not just intellectuals but activists and, in the case of García Linera, later formed part of the political party that gained state power.

Under these conditions, a new social movement had emerged demanding new forms of participation and direct democracy with cross-sectoral, class, gender, generational and ethnic alliances (Assies 2003). Indeed, these new social movements, in all of their complexity, required scholars to go beyond "an economistic form of class analysis that ignores the subjective aspects of class formation on the one hand, and an overall subjectivist and idealist postmodernist interpretation on the other" (Veltmeyer 1997: 149). In a similar vein, Arsel, Akbulut and Adaman (2015: 391) argue that understanding new environmental struggles that build on cross-class alliances require "a more flexible understanding of class that goes beyond direct relationship to production and distribution of economic surplus" to one that gives primacy to exclusion. Using a case study from another part of the world, they reveal how a unique coalition of peasant activists and an NGO formed in Turkey based not on their shared class positions but on their shared forms of resource and political exclusion. The environmentalism of the peasants and what Arsel, Akbulut and Adaman (2015: 376) call the "environmentalism of the malcontent" produced a mutually beneficial collaboration similar to the convergence of social movements, NGOs and intellectuals that began with the Water War in Cochabamba through to the election of Evo Morales and MAS. Austerity measures brought on by neoliberal policies only ignited the subjective self-awareness of the marginalized, exploited and excluded classes. Women, youth, Indigenous Peoples, peasants, rural and urban workers, NGOs and intellectuals alike gained strength in the collective unity of their subjective identities based in their broader position as the excluded and marginalized classes.

The movement, or convergence of movements, remained vibrant as the Gas War, a conflict that erupted over the control of Bolivia's natural gas reserves throughout the next five years and peaked in 2003, led to the resignation of two presidents and ultimately the election of Bolivia's first Indigenous president, Evo Morales, and MAS. Nearly 60 percent of the population was impoverished by the mid-2000s and over one-third lived in extreme poverty, signalling the exclusion and marginalization of the Bolivian majority (Weisbrot, Ray and Johnston 2009). Neoliberal governments that had held state power for the previous twenty years had finally reached a crisis of legitimacy that could no longer be reconciled with the kinds of residual fixes inherent in neoliberal social reformism (Assies 2000) or neoliberal multiculturalism (Hale 2002). The new social movement alliances represented a political shift as the excluded and marginalized became a powerful united majority against neoliberalism, triggered by a cognitive liberation of combined class and ethnic consciousness and reinforced through political participation that partially dismantled the pre-existing unequal structures of power. Promising to restore Bolivia's sovereignty over its natural resources and redistribute the country's wealth to the marginalized majority with a new vision of communitarian socialism, Morales and MAS gained their legitimacy through support from the Pacto de Unidad while discursively ostracizing the oligarchic and economic elites and launching an agrarian revolution.

The Agrarian Revolution: Reclaiming State Legitimacy

In June 2006, President Evo Morales announced the beginning of an agrarian revolution in the lowlands of Santa Cruz — a region dominated by large-scale agro-industrialists and the country's economic elites. With thousands of supporters, including Indigenous Peoples, peasants and rural wage labourers, President Morales presented 60 Indigenous communities with communal land titles (TCOs) representing over 7.5 million hectares (Fabricant 2012). Although this represented important formal recognitions of territorial rights for Indigenous communities, it should not be confused with (re)distribution, as these communities had already occupied and controlled those lands that had been inactive in the National Institute for Agrarian Reform (Instituto Nacional de la Reforma Agraria, INRA) database for the previous ten years. Promising that an additional 20 million hectares would be distributed to Bolivia's 2.5 million rural poor over the next five years, President Morales exclaimed, "The great landowners of the Oriente are crying. They are hysterically crying because they know that their glory days are over.... We will seize their unproductive land and give it to poor *campesinos*!" (quoted in Fabricant 2012: 140). Five months later, Law 3545 (*Reconducción Comunitaria de la Reforma Agraria*) was enacted, formally launching the agrarian revolution.

The principle objectives of the agrarian revolution under Law 3545 are (1) to ensure that all land serves a socioeconomic function; (2) to redefine the terms of expropriation of medium- and large-scale landholdings for the public good and to ensure the Indigenous communities have access to sufficient land-based resources for their sustainable reproduction; (3) to redefine the terms and prioritize the distribution of public lands for Indigenous and peasant communities; (4) and to reform INRA, which had lacked institutional legitimacy during the neoliberal period, with increased transparency and execution to transform the agrarian structure (INRA 2010).

Despite a very progressive and radical discourse, the agrarian revolution in Bolivia is better characterized as a formalization process of land tenure relations than redistributive agrarian reform. The application of the Social Economic Function (*Función Económica y Social*) attempts to encourage people to invest for "an efficient, dynamic and growing agriculture" (Byres 2004: 3). Rather than imposing land size ceilings on operational holdings as is necessary for any redistributive land reform, loopholes in the legislation have virtually eliminated land ceilings altogether. The gap between state discourse and practice is part and parcel of MAS's political strategy to maintain state power through the balancing of popular legitimating discourses of resource wealth distribution and the continued accumulation of capital via an extractivist development model.

One of the main purposes of Law 3545 was to extend the period of *saneamiento,* which had expired in October 2006 under Law 1715. From 1996 to 2006, the *saneamiento* managed to formally title only approximately 12 percent of the roughly 107 million hectares of total rural (public and private) lands that were to be regularized during this period (INRA 2010). Despite this shortcoming, important advances for Indigenous rights were established through the designation of autonomous and communally owned Indigenous TCOs. Bolivia's Constitution of 1994 and Law 1715 legislated the recognition of "inalienable, indivisible, irreversible, collective" TCOs that "may exercise administrative and judicial functions in accordance to their own norms, practices and procedures, provided they are not contrary to the Constitution and existing laws" (Article 171, Constitution of Bolivia 1994). From 1996 to 2006, over 8 million hectares were formally recognized and titled as TCOs, representing an impressive 64 percent of the total amount of land titled during this period, yet a far cry from the 16.4 million hectares of TCOs that were to be recognized by INRA during these ten years (Colque, Tinta and Sanjinés 2016).

From 2006 to 2009, the MAS government claimed to have titled and regularized[5] over 30 million hectares of public and private land — tripling in just four years what was achieved in the ten-year duration of Law 1715 (INRA 2010). While this is indeed impressive, it should be noted that nearly half (15 million hectares) of the total was titled as public land (*tierras fiscales*), while some 19 million hectares were already in the process and carried over from the pre-2006 period (Colque, Tinta and Sanjinés 2016). The formalization of public lands does not mean that public lands were distributed, but rather that they were titled and registered as public rather than private or protected lands. These, of course, may be subject to distributive reforms in the future, though many are located on forested lands and areas not suitable for cultivation (Colque, Tinta and Sanjinés 2016). Nonetheless, the state was able to use the figure of 31 million hectares to increase its legitimacy through public discourse without actually challenging the existing agrarian structure through zero-sum land-based transfers of wealth. Expropriation, or reversion, of unproductive *latifundios* in terms of the technical-legal criteria was not applied, but rather "used selectively as a political tool against certain Bolivian opposition leaders considered to be separatists" — namely conservative landowning political activists Branko Marinkovic and Osvaldo Monasterio (Urioste 2012: 453).

This politically contentious period represents an important political conjuncture in which the historically marginalized masses represented by the Pacto de Unidad had become part of, and appeared represented by, state institutions. A renewed sense of class and identity politics reinvigorated Indigenous and peasant populations in particular as they were, in large part, responsible for the rise of Morales and MAS after years of struggle against the neoliberal reforms of the previous two decades. The country's economic elites, on the other hand, could no longer count on state managers and their institutions to support their economic interests. Populist discourses of resource nationalization and the agrarian revolution rendered their future uncertain, prompting a coalition between the Media Luna[6] led by Santa Cruz governor and opposition leader Rubén Costas. Divisions within the country became increasingly stark and visible — between the highlands and lowlands, Indigenous and mestizo, classes of labour and capital. After the oppositional forces of the Media Luna pushed for autonomy, a national recall referendum was held in August 2008, with results showing overwhelming (67 percent) support for President Evo Morales and Vice President Alvaro García Linera. In September, violent protests erupted throughout the country as the "autonomist right" led by Costas attempted a civic coup by occupying and burning public institutions across the country, including INRA — ultimately coming to a halt after the Porvenir massacre, in which clashes between the right-wing civic movement and MAS supporters led to the deaths of nineteen people and many more wounded (UNASUR 2008). The state mobilized the armed forces and, with widespread support among its social bases, retook control over its public institutions and successfully demobilized the oppositional forces and their attempted coup d'état. For García Linera (2011: 22), this was the point of bifurcation, a "clash of material forces," that solidified MAS's control over state power through the mobilization and support of societal forces, effectively forcing the opposition to retreat.

Although the political opposition, led by Jorge Quiroga and the Social Democratic Power (*Poder Democrático Social*) party, was in decline, they still held a majority in the Senate, signalling some negotiating power in the final version of the 2009 Political Constitution of the State. Of particular significance for the politics of agrarian change is the revision of Article 315 concerning the maximum land-size ceiling of 5,000 hectares. In previous drafts of the Constitution developed with the social movements of the National Coordination for Change, "it was decided that no one, by any means, could have landholdings larger than 5000 hectares" (Francescone 2012: 68). The final version of the Constitution states that the land ceiling is not applied retroactively (meaning existing landholdings over 5,000 hectares are legal) and that the 5,000 hectares land ceiling applies to each individual associate (meaning a company can easily fix its associate-to-land ratio), effectively rendering the land ceiling inapplicable (McKay and Colque 2016). In fact, the unaltered legalization of GM soybean seeds, and the more recent legislation that increases deforestation limits (Law 741), pardons previous unauthorized deforestation (Law 739) and extends regulatory inspections for the *Función Económica y Social* from two to five years (Law 740), are quite telling. The agrarian revolution is, in fact, not transforming the highly unequal agrarian structure, and is better described as a tenurial reform designed to render rural areas more legible while facilitating continued control over land-based natural resources by the agro-industrial and landowning elites.

The question, therefore, is how to interpret and understand the politics behind these processes and the state-society-capital dynamics after the point of bifurcation that had seemingly solidified MAS's control over state power. Castañón Ballivián (2015) suggests that it was around this time that the Santa Cruz elite sought an alliance with MAS rather than continued conflict. Rather than be excluded politically, they decided it was in their best interests to become part of MAS's Process of Change (*Proceso de Cambio*). In a more recent piece of work, Webber (2017: 339) reiterates this argument with the notion of an "agro-capital-state alliance" that emerged in 2010 and "the rupture in the relationship between the government and lowland indigenous organizations." This rupture was further exacerbated when the government approved the construction of a highway through a protected area and TCO in 2011, officially dissolving the Pacto de Unidad and the strong state-society relations that had brought Morales and MAS to state power in 2006. Still, questions remain as to why MAS would abandon their plans for an agrarian revolution and form an alliance with agro-capitalists rather than support their main constituents represented by Indigenous, *originario* and peasant groups. The next chapter analyzes the politics of agrarian change under Morales and MAS as capital-intensive production becomes ubiquitous, transforming agrarian social relations through new forms of exclusion and control.

NOTES

1. Parts of this chapter have been published in McKay and Colque (2016).
2. In 1979 the National Confederation of Peasant Workers of Bolivia was restructured into the Unified Confederation of Peasants of Bolivia (Confederación Sindical Única de Trabajadores Campesinos de Bolivia) and became much more autonomous in terms of its relation with the state (Albó 2002: 77).
3. For Kay and Urioste (2007), "the 1953 law legitimated disguised forms of neo-latifundism, under the generic heading of 'enterprise.'"
4. Many of Bolivian president Hugo Banzer's economic advisors were educated at the Harvard Kennedy School and travelled to Cambridge in the spring of 1985 for a seminar with Harvard economist Jeffrey Sachs, who then became an economic advisor for Bolivian president Paz Estenssoro's New Economic Plan (Conaghan et al. 1990).
5. This refers to parcels, known as *saneadas*, in the last stages of formalization for title.
6. "Media Luna" (half-moon) refers to the geographic shape of a group of four departments in Bolivia (Pando, Beni, Santa Cruz and Tarija) that were controlled by the opposition upon the election of MAS in 2006.

REFERENCES

Albó, Xavier. 2002. "Bolivia: From Indian and Campesino Leaders to Councillor and Parliamentary Deputies." In Rachel Sieder (ed.), *Multiculturalism in Latin America: Indigenous Rights, Diversity and Democracy*. New York: Palgrave Macmillan.

ANAPO. 2015. *Memoria Anual 2015*. Santa Cruz: Asociacion de Productores de Oleaginosas y Trigo.

Arsel, Murat, Bengi Akbulut, and Fikret Adaman. 2015. "Environmentalism of the Malcontent: Anatomy of an Anti-Coal Power Plant Struggle in Turkey." *Journal of Peasant Studies*, 42 (April). Taylor & Francis: 371–395.

Assies, Willem. 2000. "El Constitucionalismo Multietnico En America Latina: El Caso de Bolivia." In *XII Congreso Internacional "Derecho Consuetudinario y Pluralismo Legal: Desafíos En El Tercer Milenio*. Arica, Chile.

____. 2003. "David versus Goliath in Cochabamba: Water Rights, Neoliberalism, and the Revival of Social Protest in Bolivia." *Latin American Perspectives*, 30, 130: 14–36.

Barber, R.G., M. Orellana, F. Navarro, O. Diaz, and M.A. Soruco. 1996. "Effects of Conservation and Conventional Tillage Systems after Land Clearing on Soil Properties and Crop Yield in Santa Cruz, Bolivia." *Soil & Tillage Research*, 38: 133–152.

Byres, Terence J. 2004. "Introduction: Contextualizing and Interrogating the GKI Case for Redistributive Land Reform." *Journal of Agrarian Change*, 4, 1–2: 1–16.

Castañón Ballivián, Enrique. 2015. "Discurso Empresarial vs. Realidad Campesina: La Ecología Política de La Producción de Soya En Santa Cruz, Bolivia." *Cuestión Agraria*, 2, 1: 65–86.

Colque, Gonzalo, Efraín Tinta, and Esteban Sanjinés. 2016. *Segunda Reforma Agraria: Una Historia Que Incomoda*. La Paz: TIERRA.
Conaghan, Catherine M., James M. Malloy, and Luis A. Abugattas. 1990. "Business and the 'Boys': The Politics of Neoliberalism in the Central Andes." *Latin American Research Review*, 25, 2: 3–30.
Fabricant, Nicole. 2012. *Mobilizing Bolivia's Displaced: Indigenous Politics & the Struggle Over Land*. Chapel Hill, NC: University of North Carolina Press.
Francescone, Kirsten. 2012. "Paths of Development in Bolivia: Contradictions of the Proceso de Cambio." Ottawa: Carleton University.
García Linera, Álvaro. 2011. "Las Tensiones Creativas de La Revolución," 1–27. <http://www.rebelion.org/docs/134332.pdf>.
Gramsci, Antonio. 1971. *Selections from the Prison Notebooks of Antonio Gramsci*. Edited by Quintin Hoare and Geoffrey Nowell Smith. London: Lawrence and Wishart.
Grindle, Merilee. 2000. *Audacious Reforms: Institutional Invention and Democracy in Latin America*. Baltimore and London: Johns Hopkins University Press.
Hale, Charles R. 2002. "Does Multiculturalism Menace? Governance, Cultural Rights and the Politics of Identity in Guatemala." *Journal of Latin American Studies*, 34, 3: 485–524.
INE. 2015. *Primer Censo Agropecuario 2013*. La Paz.
INRA. 2010. *La Tierra Vuelve a Manos Indigenas y Campesinas. Instituto Nacional de Reforma Agraria*. La Paz: INRA.
Kay, Cristóbal. 2009. "Development Strategies and Rural Development: Exploring Synergies, Eradicating Poverty." *Journal of Peasant Studies*, 36, 1: 103–137.
Kay, Cristóbal, and Miguel Urioste. 2007. "Bolivia's Unfinished Agrarian Reform: Rural Poverty and Development Policies." In A.H. Akram-Lodhi, S.M. Borras, and Cristóbal Kay (eds.), *Land, Poverty and Livelihoods in the Era of Globalization: Perspectives from Developing and Transition Countries*. London and New York: Routledge.
Klein, Herbert S. 2011. *A Consice History of Bolivia*. Cambridge: Cambridge University Press.
Malloy, James M. 1970. *Bolivia: The Uncompleted Revoltuion*. Pittsburgh: University of Pittsburgh Press.
McKay, Ben, and Gonzalo Colque. 2016. "Bolivia's Soy Complex: The Development of 'Productive Exclusion.'" *Journal of Peasant Studies*, 43, 2: 583–610.
Müller, Robert, Till Pistorius, Sophia Rohde, Gerhard Gerold, and Pablo Pacheco. 2013. "Policy Options to Reduce Deforestation Based on a Systematic Analysis of Drivers and Agents in Lowland Bolivia." *Land Use Policy*, 30, 1: 895–907.
Sanabria, Harry. 1999. "Consolidating States, Restructuring Economies, and Confronting Workers and Peasants: The Antinomies of Bolivian Neoliberalism." *Comparative Studies in Society and History*, 41, 3: 535–562.
Scott, James C. 1998. *Seeing Like a State*. New Haven: Yale University Press.
Thorn, Richard S. 1971. "The Economic Transformation." In James M. Malloy and Richard S. Thorn (eds.), *Beyond the Revolution: Bolivia since 1952*. Pittsburgh: University of Pittsburgh Press.
UNASUR. 2008. *Informe de La Commission de UNASUR Sobre Los Sucesos de Pando:*

Hacia Un Alba de Justicia Para Bolivia. Quito.
Urioste, Miguel. 2007. *La Revolución Agraria de Evo Morales*. La Paz: Fundación TIERRA.
____. 2012. "Concentration and 'Foreignisation' of Land in Bolivia." *Canadian Journal of Development Studies/Revue Canadienne d'études Du Développement*, 33, 4: 439–457.
Valdivia, G. 2010. "Agrarian Capitalism and Struggles over Hegemony in the Bolivian Lowlands." *Latin American Perspectives*, 37, 4: 67–87.
Van Dijck, P. 1998. "Economic Transformation and Policy Reform: Shocks and Balances." In P. Van Dijck (ed.), *The Bolivian Experiment: Structural Adjustment and Poverty Alleviation*. Amsterdam: CEDLA.
Veltmeyer, Henry. 1997. "New Social Movements in Latin America: The Dynamics of Class and Identity." *Journal of Peasant Studies*, 25, 1: 139–169.
Vos, R., L. Haeduck, and J.A. Mejia. 1998. "Structural Adjustment and Poverty." In P. Van Dijck (ed.), *The Bolivian Experiment: Structural Adjustment and Poverty Alleviation*. Amsterdam: CEDLA.
Webber, Jeffery R. 2017. "Evo Morales, *Transformismo*, and the Consolidation of Agrarian Capitalism in Bolivia." *Journal of Agrarian Change*, 17, 2: 330–347.
Weisbrot, Mark, Rebecca Ray, and Jake Johnston. 2009. *Bolivia: The Economy During the Morales Administration. CEPR Reports and Issue Briefs*. Washington, DC.
World Bank. 1998. *Eastern Lowlands: Natural Resource Management and Agricultural Production Project*. Washington, DC: World Bank.
Zavaleta Mercado, René. 1986. *Lo Nacional-Popular En Bolivia*. México: Sigo Veintiuno.

3 State Control: The Politics of Agrarian Change

> Just imagine if the people here wanted to block roads and destroy the main transportation links for soybeans and other products. It would put so much pressure on the government. But that doesn't happen because smallholders have become chained and dependent on agro-industry; therefore, they want to see it succeed. If they block roads it will immediately have negative impacts on their livelihoods. People here live from harvest to harvest, so to mobilize against the same industry for which they now depend is against their best interest.
>
> — *Roberto Churata, co-founder of CAPPO, an association of small-scale farmers*

The many contradictions that exist regarding Bolivia's agricultural development model in the context of state rhetoric about an agrarian revolution, a Law of Mother Nature and commitment to food sovereignty (McKay, Nehring and Walsh-Dilley 2014) reflect the broader process of what Webber (2011) describes as reconstituted neoliberalism. This process is characterized by social and economic policy changes at the margins without major structural changes to the political economy (Brabazon and Webber 2014). State rhetoric has become more of a legitimating discourse (Kersson 2013) than a structural transformation, while key social movements have been co-opted by the state, resulting in a loss of autonomy and lack of empowerment among those in the movements (McKay, Nehring and Walsh-Dilley 2014). As Brabazon and Webber (2014: 461–462) point out, the trajectory of agrarian change in Bolivia is "reinforcing rather than dismantling the concentration of quality productive land amongst medium- and large-scale agrarian capitalists." Instead of breaking with the past, state policies have actually "reproduced dependency relationships with agro-industrial capital" (Cordoba and Jansen 2014: 497), thereby not providing any alternative pathways for small farmers or peasants through "neocollectivist agrarian development." These policies have reinforced a model attuned to the World Bank's (2007) proposed pathways out of poverty, which are three: (1) advance as capitalist farmers within the agro-industrial system, (2) become rural wage labourers working on or off the farm, or (3) migrate to the city.

This chapter analyzes the politics of agrarian change throughout the contemporary period with a focus on the relations between the state, its main constituents represented by the major social movements of the Pacto de Unidad and various class fractions of capital. New political dynamics, alliances, tensions and conflicts within and among these entities have important implications for trajectories of agrarian change in Bolivia and must be understood in the context of a socially progressive leftist government that came to power promising an agrarian revolution.

The "Productive Revolution": A State-Capital Alliance

When MAS took state power in 2006 it was highly dependent upon support from the Pacto de Unidad. In fact, many of the leaders of the organizations of the Pacto were also MAS leaders and thus became absorbed into key positions within state institutions. Although related social movements may not have been completely co-opted by the state, they certainly lost much of their autonomy as their leaders entered into a very close and mutually beneficial relationship with MAS (sometimes for personal over organizational gain). Forming a strong state-society relation in this particular sense, MAS was able to gain and maintain legitimacy by working closely with key leaders of the Pacto who would then extend the state's legitimacy via the dispersion of social expenditures to their regional and municipal organizational factions. By way of absorbing the Pacto within the Constituent Assembly, MAS was able to develop strong relationships with constituents across the country, particularly the Indigenous and peasant populations in rural areas, primarily through clientelistic measures. With support and participation from leftist intellectual groups such as the Comuna and Duende, including then vice president Álvaro García Linera and economic and finance minister Luis Arce Catacora, MAS put forth a New Economic, Social, Communitarian and Productive Model (*Nuevo Modelo Económico, Social, Comunitario y Productivo*), which was to challenge the neoliberal model and lead to a structural transformation of the political economy.

According to the former finance minister, Luis Arce Catacora (2015), Bolivia's economic model is based on four pillars: (1) growth and development based on the use of natural resource to benefit Bolivians, (2) appropriation of the economic surplus, (3) redistribution of the extractivist rents, and (4) reduction of inequality and poverty. Essentially, surpluses generated (largely through rent) from strategic sectors (which include hydrocarbons, mining, electricity and natural resources) are to be transferred to sectors that supposedly generate income and employment (which include industrial and artisanal manufacturing, tourism, agricultural development, housing, commerce, transportation and other service sectors). The state, framed as a Weberian-type fully autonomous and capable bureaucratic entity, is seen as the central actor in this economic model designated to redistribute extractivist rents in order to foster industrialization, thereby retaining surplus value production, generating employment and overcoming the reliance on raw material exports. The "redistributive state" also uses its revenues for inequality and poverty reduction through cash transfer programs that include Bono Juancito Pinto,[1] Renta Dignidad[2] and Bono Juana Azurduy.[3] For García Linera (2012), then vice president, the Bolivian state is pursuing an extractivist development model to enable it to redistribute its natural resource wealth and overcome extractivism itself.

Despite the stated intentions to challenge the neoliberal economic model and pursue a structural transformation towards a socialist society (Arce Catacora 2015), severe shortcomings have led to processes of exclusion, value appropriation by a concentrated agro-industrial oligopoly and new forms of economic, social and environmental extraction that further threaten historically marginalized populations. Agricultural development, which is supposed to be an income- and employment-generating sector according to the economic model, has done just the opposite. The agro-industrial bias and capital-intensive soy complex excludes the rural majority and is controlled by a market oligopoly that appropriates the majority of the surplus generated. Further, Bolivia's primary product exports increased under the Morales administration, while the production of industrial value-added goods (heavy machinery) and processing take place abroad. According to the model, labour should move out of agriculture and into industry, but the lack of forward and backward linkages and sectoral articulation associated with the soy complex renders labour surplus to the needs of capital accumulation. The lack of structural change has led to the persistence of primary export dependence and an economic model in which extractivist rents are captured by political and economic elites while legitimacy is maintained through cash transfers to the poor facilitated by favourable commodity prices.

The commodities boom of the early 2000s combined with the partial nationalization of key sectors of the economy increased the state's budget by some 445 percent — from US$5.9 billion in 2005 to US$32.1 billion in 2015[4] (MEFP 2015). During the same period, public investment increased from US$629 million in 2005 to US$6.179 billion — an impressive 882 percent increase. These massive increases in the state's budget have increased the capacity of state managers and institutions to simultaneously fulfil both its accumulation and legitimization functions (O'Connor 1973).

While the fiscal capacity of the Bolivian state has led to substantial absolute increases in public expenditures across all sectors,[5] the average social sector investment over the ten years from 2005 to 2015 actually decreased from 30 to 27 percent, while an estimate based on preliminary data for 2016 shows a drop to 20 percent (MEFP 2015). The vast majority of public investment is allocated to energy and hydrocarbon development (40 percent) and transportation infrastructure (29 percent), which together account for nearly 70 percent of the public investment budget for 2016 (MEFP 2015).

As a percentage of GDP, gross national savings have averaged 25.3 percent since 2006, while total investments have averaged only 17.6 percent (World Bank 2016a; Quandl 2016). In a developing country like Bolivia, which lacks robust value-added industrial and manufacturing sectors (forward and backward linkages) and a home market in agriculture, as well as a more specialized, skilled and educated workforce, such a high savings-investment ratio constrains productive transformation. According to Jayati Ghosh (2015: 11), when domestic savings are higher than investment there is "a process of squeezing out savings from the population as a whole but not investing it within the economy to ensure future growth." Ghosh argues that developing countries (and most primary-producing export-oriented economies) should not have a high savings-to-investment ratio, as this signals a lack of investment in economic diversification for productive transformation, particularly in value-added industries and education (Ghosh 2015). Bolivia's international reserves have increased almost 400 percent since MAS came to power — from US$3.178 billion in 2006 to US$15.123 billion in 2014 (BCB 2016). International reserves do help fend off financial crises, but the lack of investment in diversifying the economy and educating a skilled workforce perpetuates dependence on export-oriented extractive enclaves, which are more susceptible to volatile international commodities markets. Thus, while it is important to maintain a comfortable level of reserves when transitioning away from commodity market dependence, maintaining a savings-investment ratio as high as Bolivia's unnecessarily deprives the economy and population from much-needed investment in productive, value-added transformation.

Bolivia's state expenditures reveal the priority of social capital investments to serve accumulation interests, particularly in the extractive sectors, though without enough emphasis on developing forward and backward, value-added linkages with a highly skilled and productive workforce. Yet developing such intersectoral linkages does not seem a priority for Bolivia's capitalist elites or the state. Capitalist elites are invested in extractive sectors (mining, hydrocarbons and soybeans) and thus are interested in extraction, rents and external markets for export. State actors remain interested in political power and thus balancing the economic interests of capital while maintaining social harmony among the masses. This requires maintaining economic stability for extractivist interests, fending off potential economic crises with high savings and reserves and redistributing some of the resource wealth through cash transfers to the marginalized and excluded through social expenses and welfare. This neo-extractivist development model enables both the state and capital to benefit from the fruits of the extractive sector. But while the partial nationalization of the extractive sectors has allowed the state to collect more rents, "they end up reproducing the same productive processes, similar relations of power, and the same social and environmental impacts" that private or foreign control do (Gudynas 2010: 12). These dynamics have enabled a state-capital alliance to emerge with mutually reinforcing accumulation interests while the initial state-society relations with MAS and the Pacto de Unidad and the expanded and increased social sector investments have contributed to the state's legitimacy.

After the 2009 general elections, Evo Morales and MAS won a convincing 64.2 percent of the vote and, for the first time, controlled both the lower (Chamber of Deputies) and upper house (Senate) of the Plurinational Legislative Assembly with a two-thirds (absolute) majority. Yet, instead of pursuing structural reforms, they continued with a model of development based on neo-extractivist logic. In the agrarian sector, agricultural development has taken the form of "agrarian extractivism," with economic, social and ecological forms of extraction that are similar to those in traditional extractivist sectors such as mining and hydrocarbons (McKay 2017). In June 2011, Law 144 for a "productive revolution" (*Ley de la Revolución Productiva Comunitaria Agropecuaria*) was enacted with the principal objective of achieving "food sovereignty" and establishing the institutional, political, technical and financial capacity for increased production, transformation and commercialization of agricultural and forestry product.

While Law 144 is filled with popular and inclusive language for a pathway towards food sovereignty — such as communitarian and organic production, the recuperation of soils and native seeds and respect for Mother Earth for *vivir bien* (good living) — the lack of structural reforms, including redistributive agrarian reform, the increased dependence on food imports for food security and the continued concentration of control over land-based natural resources and decision-making have eroded the possibilities to develop pathways towards food sovereignty in practice (McKay, Nehring and Walsh-Dilley 2014: 1193). Even the development of the soy complex and expansion of the agricultural frontier — principally for export-oriented agro-industrial flex crops — is now being framed as a form of food sovereignty and food security, despite the obvious contradictions and the substantially increased dependency on food staple imports (Vicepresidente 2012). Despite being a net food exporter, Bolivia remains dependent on imports for staple foods for household consumption (INE 2015a). Food imports increased some 62 percent from 2010 to 2014, while food import prices jumped a disproportionate 92 percent (IBCE 2016; Quispe 2015). Further, currency devaluations in neighbouring Argentina and Brazil have also enabled their producers' products to undercut Bolivia's small-scale traditional crop producers (Quispe 2015). This is due, in large part, to the agro-industrial bias of the productive revolution, which lacks effective support for the majority of Bolivian farmers. Rather than any meaningful changes in terms of access and control over resources and decision making processes, the productive revolution is rooted in a new institutional economics approach which attempts to minimize market imperfections, connect farmers to market-based mechanisms, increase productivity and efficiency particularly through the establishment of recognized and enforceable private property rights.

To support small-scale farmers with input-supply and market access with just prices, the state-run public procurement company, EMAPA (*Empresa de Apoyo a la Producción de Alimentos,* EMAPA), was established. However, EMAPA has been severely constrained by its lack of capacity and implementation failures as it excludes the most marginal producers and reinforces a model of intensive agriculture as a way forward which is not suitable for the majority of the small-scale producers it claims to support (Cordoba and Jansen 2014). For Roberto Churata, one of the founders of the Chamber of Small Farmers of the East (Cámara de Pequeños Productores del Oriente, CAPPO), the region's largest small farmer association with 15,000 members, EMAPA "has no vision, and suffers from a lack of planning .... it does not function" (personal interview, San Julián, January 2015). Churata explained how EMAPA should be cooperatively owned and operated by the farmers in the region, not by the central state, because "they don't have the proper people running the industry" (personal interview, San Julián, January 2015). As Cordoba and Jansen (2014: 497) conclude, EMAPA has, perhaps paradoxically, facilitated "the integration of small producers into this internationalizing agro-industrial complex" which reproduce relationships of debt and dependency with agro-industrial capital.

These market-based, residual approaches to poverty reduction view poverty "as a consequence of being 'left out' of processes of development, on the assumption that development brings economic growth which, sooner or later, raises everybody's income" (Bernstein 1992: 24). With this approach the policies of the productive revolution have failed to address the underlying relational aspects of poverty and marginalization in terms of the social relations of production and reproduction as well as property and power (Bernstein 1992: 24). Without challenging the unequal agrarian structure, Bolivia's agricultural development policies have reinforced and reproduced the existing dominant forms of (agro-industrial) production and the concentration of resource wealth and control through new mechanisms of exclusion.

Mechanisms of Social and Economic Exclusion

Highland peasants already settled in Santa Cruz and highland peasants seeking land access in the soybean expansion zone are confronted with a new situation in which the mechanisms of access to land and agro-capital are more complex and inherently exclusive to those with certain access mechanisms[6] while excluding the capital-less workforce. The majority of those who were fortunate to gain a small parcel during the previous "march to the east," despite being small-scale landowners, lack other access mechanisms to advance as small-scale capitalist producers due to their dependence on agribusiness in terms of access to technology, capital and markets. Rural people, especially the poor, seeking land access are not only excluded from land (as it now sells for $2,000–$5,000 per hectare) but also no longer required as cheap labour since the model of production has changed from labour intensive to capital intensive. Access mechanisms for production have thus been "appropriated" by agro-industry, requiring farmers to integrate with industrial value-chain agriculture to work the land. Yet, in order to integrate, smallholders are, in effect, excluded from production since they need to hire out all land-related services (sowing, fumigating, harvesting) and enter into a contract for inputs from agro-industry. Access mechanisms thus become mechanisms of social and economic exclusion, leading to relations of debt and dependency, contradictory class positions, and social differentiation.

Migration flows and workforce dynamics over time demonstrate the trends towards urban-rural migration. Data suggests that migration to the lowlands has decreased substantially, along with the labour force employed in the agricultural sector (INE 2001; 2012a). According to census data, the share of the economically active population has decreased in the heart of the soybean expansion zone over the past twenty years. In Cuatro Cañadas, the share of the economically active population in agriculture has decreased from 83.1 percent in 1992 to 45.1 percent in 2012, while in San Julián the share decreased from 70 percent in 2001 to 47.3 percent in 2012 (INE 2001; 2012a). The adoption of Monsanto's glyphosate herbicide, for example, has replaced the need to hire workers. As one farmer explained to me, "We used to employ sixty to seventy people to clean the fields after harvest; now the glyphosate kills everything so we don't need to hire anybody." The development of highly mechanized agro-industrial production continues to exclude smallholders and peasants in a double sense: they are unable to access capital, technology and therefore machinery to put land into production, and they are unable to access viable labour opportunities in a highly productive rural area. This is not inherently problematic, but becomes so if this exclusion is not accompanied by other means of labour absorption elsewhere.

This data shows that the agricultural sector in Santa Cruz is based on a model that continues to grow economically and expand geographically without the need for additional labour supply (Colque 2014). One important qualitative feature that this quantitative data does not reveal is the differentiation of smallholders. Official data considers those who lease their lands as "small farmers" — but they are not engaging in productive activity as the capital-intensive model has rendered them subject to processes of productive exclusion. This is a situation where the fundamental problem is not a direct dispossession of land, but the denial of access to agro-capital for small-scale landholders and the separation of the workforce from the accumulation dynamics of agrarian capitalism.

The Partida Arrangement: A New Mechanism of Exclusion

With the official adoption of GM seeds in 2005, the mechanization of soybean production has intensified and what was once a labour-intensive agrarian production region has become dominated by capital-intensive production. Thousands of hectares can now be cultivated by just a few workers, as massive mechanized seeders and harvesters (combines) work the vast monocrop plantations. Despite the high investment requirements to participate in this type of agricultural production, small-scale farmers are both pushed and pulled into the soy complex due to pressures to "modernize," favourable prices during the commodities boom and the widespread use of GM seeds and glyphosate fumigation. The transition to cash crop production in the soybean expansion zone of Santa Cruz is understandable. From 2005 to 2015, soybean prices doubled in Bolivia and the world's largest agro-multinationals — ADM, Bunge, Cargill and Louis Dreyfus, among others —moved in, controlling vast market shares of Bolivia's storage, processing and export markets while using marketing mechanisms to lure smallholders into the soy complex (ANAPO 2015; AEMP 2013). However, the manner in which small farmers participate in soy production is much different than statistical data suggests.

Among soybean producers in Santa Cruz, for example, large-scale farmers (those with over 1,000 hectares), who represent just 2 percent of the total farmers, control some 71 percent of the land, while small-scale farmers (those with 50 hectares or less), who represent 78 percent of total farmers, control just 9 percent of the land under soybean cultivation. In terms of the entire rural area in the country's fertile soybean expansion zone, small-scale farms — representing 82.9 percent of the total land titles formalized under the *saneamiento* — control just 16.9 percent of the land area, while medium- (with an average of 325.8 hectares) and large-scale farms (with an average of 1,926.8 hectares) representing 12 percent of formalized land titles control 61.6 percent of the total[7] (Colque, Tinta and Sanjinés 2016). Despite such land-based inequalities, we cannot dismiss the importance of the advances made under the Morales government in recognizing Indigenous territories (TCOs) and preventing the consolidation of what Colque, Tinta and Sanjinés (2016) call speculative estates (*latifundio especulativo*). Similarly, we cannot ignore the fact that the agrarian structure has been left largely unchanged as new forms of marginalization, exclusion and debt relations exacerbate existing rural inequalities (McKay and Colque 2016; McKay 2018).

Despite the unequal landholding structure, this data suggests that soybean production does provide a livelihood for 11,000 small farmers and their families. While this is in some ways true, a deeper understanding of the soy complex reveals a more complicated story with highly exclusionary dynamics. Today, production in the two principal municipalities in Bolivia's soybean expansion zone, Cuatro Cañadas and San Julián, is completely dependent on capital-intensive mechanization — something that an estimated 86 percent of small farmers lack (Suárez, Camburn and Crespo 2010). Production requires access to heavy machinery such as a tractor, sower, harvester, fumigator and transport truck, among other inputs such as GM seeds and chemical-based fertilizers, pesticides and herbicides. For small-scale farmers, this requires either entering into some form of contract agreement or accessing credit from a financial institution. Since the land law prohibits small farmers (those with less than 50 hectares) from using their land as an asset to secure a loan, they are considered risky clientele and credit rates for them are extremely high. This leaves few options for small farmers but to enter into a contract agreement with large-scale agro-industry or with other farmers with access to machinery. But while the former option still requires renting tractors, harvesters and fumigators, the latter offers a more secure sow-to-harvest service.

The land law also prohibits landowners from renting out their land, meaning that the land is only for those who work it. For capital-poor small farmers, however, this is quite difficult given the high investment costs of production. Small farmers are therefore resorting to what is known as a *partida* arrangement, where one party supplies the land and the other the equipment and inputs. This form of land leasing was not practiced before the soybean boom but has now become common in the lowlands, where land is relatively scarce. *Partida* or *al partir* means to share or split harvest or usufruct benefits among those working the land and those who hold tenure rights to the land. The suppliers of land, in this case the small farmers, usually receive 18 to 25 percent of the harvest, but this is ultimately based on negotiation between the two parties. For small farmers, this is an attractive alternative that does not require entering into debt relations. Smallholders are not required to make any investments or rent any equipment; instead, they let someone else work their land and collect a portion of the profits after expenses. With costs of production in Bolivia's soybean expansion zone averaging $400 to $500 per hectare, the stakes are quite high for small farmers if they choose to take on the risks themselves, hoping that they do not run into problems such as drought, pests, erosion, floods and so on while also depending on yields of at least 2 tons per hectare, which over the past decade have hovered around this mark but have also been increasingly volatile due to unpredictable weather patterns (Díez 2016). Table 3.1 shows the production costs for soybean production for the summer harvest in the expansion zone based on my data.

My data from Cuatro Cañadas and San Julián show that production costs come out to US$410 per hectare. Data from the Bolivian Institute of Foreign Trade (Instituto Boliviano de Comercio Exterior) estimates soybean production costs in the summer seasons to be US$421 per hectare in the soybean expansion zone (Zone B) and US$560 per hectare in the integrated

Table 3.1 Soybean Production Costs, Expansion Zone, Summer Harvest

Inputs	US$ Per Hectare	Operations	US$ Per Hectare
Seeds	60	Soil preparation	7
Seed treatment	13	Sowing	30
Herbicides	57	Agro-chemical applications ($7 * five applications)	35
Insecticides	50	Harvest	55
Fungicides	60	Transportation ($15 per ton * 2 ton per hectare)	30
Pre-harvest desiccant	13		
Inputs total	253	Operations total	157
Total	410		

Source: Author's elaboration based on interviews in Cuatro Cañadas and San Julián

zone (Zone A) (see Figure 3.1). An average of the three provides an estimated total cost of production of US$464 per hectare of soybean cultivation. In 2008 and 2011, the price offered to producers in Bolivia for soybeans peaked at US$400 per ton. After the fall in commodities prices, soybeans decreased to a ten-year low of US$230 per ton in 2016 (ANAPO 2015, 2016). With average yields at 2 tons per hectare, producers would receive US$460 per hectare, which does not even cover the costs of production, assuming they do not have machinery and must hire services. We can also estimate the income of soybean producers during the peak years from 2008 to 2015, when prices averaged US$339 per ton. Given a minimum expected yield of 2 tons per hectare, this would generate US$678 per hectare, with profits per hectare amounting to US$214. Assuming smallholders negotiate a 25 percent return for the *partida* arrangement, they would receive US$53.50 per hectare, which, for a small-scale parcel of 50 hectares, generates an income of US$2,676.80 for the summer harvest.

In the winter harvest, many producers cultivate wheat, sunflower, sorghum or maize, as soy cultivation decreases to less than a third of the summer total (in land area and production). Yields and prices decrease substantially in the winter and, since costs of machinery and inputs are

Figure 3.1 Map of Five Zones of Agricultural Expansion in Santa Cruz, Bolivia

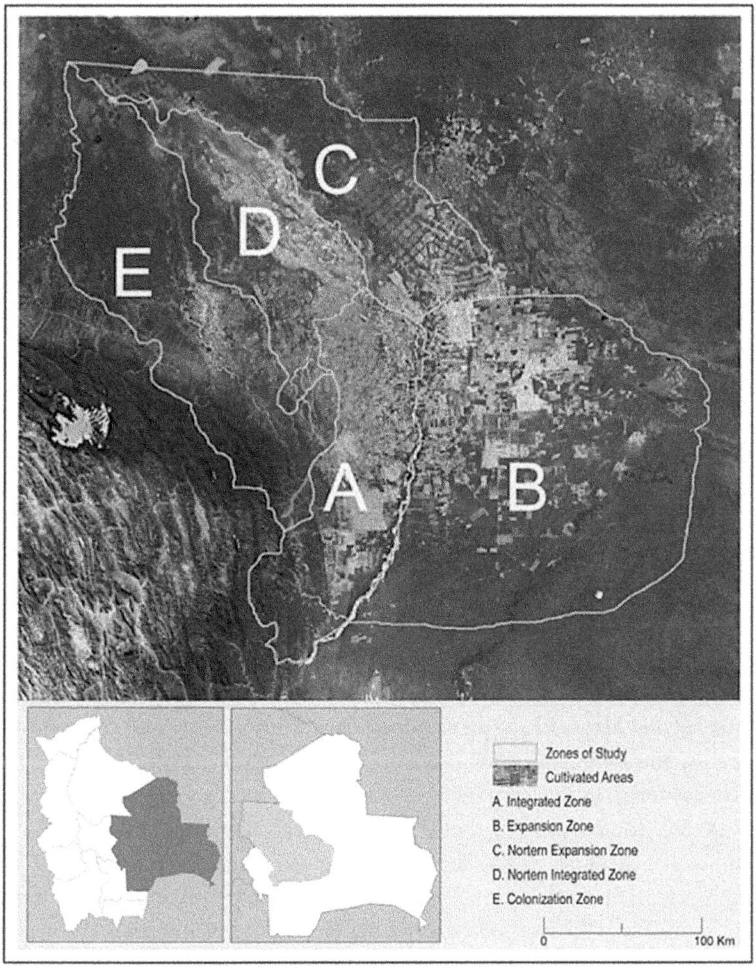

Source: McKay and Colque 2016

relatively inelastic, producers estimate that they receive 30 percent of their annual income in the winter harvest. This amounts to an annual income of US$3,830, which is US$677 more per year than the national minimum wage (INE 2016). While these estimates may seem adequate for the costs of living in rural areas, it is important to consider that these calculations assume relatively ideal conditions — in terms of the peak years of soybean prices, consistent yields and a complete 50 hectares harvest for smallholders. Nonetheless, it is primarily for these reasons that the majority of the small farmers in Cuatro Cañadas and San Julián have opted for the *partida* arrangement rather than taking the high risks associated with putting land into production.[8]

Productive Exclusion and Implications for Agrarian Change

While the *partida* arrangement may be viewed by some as a win-win, it is important to consider the implications of this trajectory of agrarian change given the new forms and relations of production and the broader political economy and ecology. First, soybean prices reached historic heights from 2008 to 2015, averaging US$339 per ton, allowing smallholders to reap the benefits of the commodities boom. According to my survey of over three hundred households, most smallholders only starting cultivating soybeans in 2010, as prices were favourable and policies and infrastructure were geared towards the soy complex. From 1996 to 2007, the decade prior to the boom, soybean prices averaged US$173 per ton. Since soybean prices have been steadily declining since peaking in 2011, it is likely the end of the commodity boom cycle and thus prices will not increase to previous peak levels on a consistent basis (World Bank 2016b).

Prices of agro-commodities such as soybeans are increasingly volatile as new financial instruments enable investors to influence prices despite being far removed from actual production, distribution and consumption — a new kind of distancing, as Jennifer Clapp (2014: 810) puts it, "by facilitating the entry of new actors taking profits along, in and around agrifood commodity chains, and by encouraging more abstraction of the commodity from its original form, in this case into a 'virtual' financial derivative product." As the global food system becomes increasingly financialized, the unpredictability of market prices escalates, rendering vulnerable those dependent on such prices. Second, the oligopoly-controlled upstream and downstream components of the soy complex and the technological and pesticide treadmill this form of production entails has increased production costs by an estimated 76 percent since 2002.[9] I elaborate on this point further in the next chapter. Third, nature has responded to the high rates of deforestation, large quantities of agro-chemicals applied to the soil and compaction due to heavy machinery with increased climate volatility, soil erosion, flooding and new weeds and pests, which contribute to the technological and pesticide treadmill. This third point is discussed further in Chapter 5.

The *partida* arrangement renders smallholders completely dependent on external factors beyond their control. Indeed, they have lost control of their land as a productive asset. The majority of those classified as small farmers are no longer agricultural producers, but class fractions of labour better characterized as semiproletarians and petty bourgeois rentiers. They are the taxi drivers, shopkeepers, bus drivers, roadside and construction workers and mechanics, among others. The transition of agricultural production from a labour-intensive to capital-intensive model has divorced, or excluded, the rural majority from accessing the factors of production. This majority is "neither dispossessed of *all* means of reproducing itself nor in possession of *sufficient* means to reproduce itself" as Bernstein (2009: 73) puts it in reference to "classes of labour." The *partida* arrangement is, in some ways, a form of disguised "proletarianisation" as described by Roger Clapp (Clapp 1988: 16) in reference to contract farming, whereby agribusiness "secures the farmer's land and labour, while leaving him/her with formal title to both" (see also Watts 1994). Smallholders in Bolivia engaging in the *partida* arrangement are indeed disguised since they are considered small-scale farmers in official government statistics yet do not actually work their land. What distinguishes the *partida* arrangement from Clapp's contract farming is that agribusiness has no need to secure control over the smallholder's labour.

As Tania Li (2011: 286) puts it, in reference to plantations in Southeast Asia that exclude local populations, "Their land is needed, but their labor is not." While land ownership is certainly still an important issue since many people depend on land rents for their income, it does not necessarily dictate the terms of control and access. Medium- and large-scale agro-capitalists have title to a certain amount of land, but many actually benefit from much more land due to *partida* arrangements with smallholders. The penetration of industrial capital and the development of the soy complex in the Bolivian lowlands is leading to a very exclusive producer environment where the need for labour has decreased substantially and the relative surplus value captured by agro-industry has increased.

This transition has several implications for not only the agrarian structure in the lowlands but also the broader rural-urban linkages concerning employment. If the majority of the 11,000 smallholders cultivating soybeans are no longer actually producing on their land, they are likely becoming disconnected from their status as a farmer. Traditional farming practices have been eroded by the adoption of high-modernist capitalist production, and the next generation of would-be family farmers are no longer learning how to produce on the family plot; they are looking to the cities for alternative opportunities. Based on my survey data, the average age of farmer heads of household is 48 years old, and the vast majority have incomplete primary education. With this demographic, level of education and rural background, the prospects for employment in urban areas are bleak. Even if youth are still interested in farming, families with four to five children are not able to make a living with a plot of less than 50 hectares within the soy complex. Medium- and large-scale agro-capitalists and large agro-industry are extending their reach, first through *partida* arrangements and later through outright land purchases.

Based on a combination of data from my household survey, Bolivia's 2013 agricultural census, key informant interviews with ANAPO's agricultural technicians and a study published by PROBIOMA, an estimated 80 to 95 percent of farmers lack complete agricultural machinery (tractor, harvester, fumigator) and therefore depend on others to work their land, either partially or completely (INE 2015b; Suárez, Camburn and Crespo 2010). The concentration of the landholding structure is not principally occurring through physical means of displacement, but rather through a gradual process of control grabbing. With the majority of the rural youth in this region looking to the urban centres, the implications for this type of agrarian transition point are a massive rural-urban migration and a reconcentration of the agrarian structure.

Given this trajectory one must question where the current and next generation of smallholders will go. Whether, where and the extent to which they will be absorbed in the urban economy is an important question worth further exploration. The capital-intensive soybean production model is not creating but eroding employment opportunities. Fearnside (2001), for example, found that soybean production in Brazil displaces eleven agricultural workers for every *one* it employs. In Bolivia, prior to mechanization, approximately ten labourers would be needed to work 1 hectare of land in a day. With mechanization, one person can sow 50 hectares in fifteen to sixteen hours, fumigate in five hours and harvest in two or three days. Labour requirements have decreased drastically, as a few people can now work several hundred hectares in a much shorter period of time. A key downfall to this technological innovation is the lack of labour opportunities and the exclusion of the majority of the rural population. If this type of creative destruction offered new employment opportunities through new types of value-added industrial development, the excluded populations could be absorbed elsewhere. However, what we observe in Bolivia is a lack of labour opportunities in the countryside with no clear pathway or opportunities in urban centres.

Employment that has been created as a result of the soy complex has tended to be precarious, seasonal, contractual and uncertain. Opportunities such as transportation during harvest, maintenance and cleaning of silos, roadside bush clearing and so on offer some employment but are tempo-

Table 3.2 Soy Complex Employment Generation, Summer Harvest

Source of Employment	Number of People Employed
Direct employment	
Farmers and agricultural workers	70,552
Agricultural commercial stores	872
Storage facilities	1,431
Processing facilities	700
Seed facilities	242
Indirect employment	
Internal transportation	20,299
Transportation for export	6,525
Total indirect	26,824
Total direct	73,797
Total direct and indirect	100,621

Sources: Suárez, Camburn and Crespo 2010.

rary, sporadic and subject to flexible arrangements. According to government data, employment in agriculture decreased from 36.8 percent in 2000 to 29.6 percent in 2011, but if we consider those actually engaged in agricultural activity the percentage would be much, much lower due to the processes of productive exclusion previously mentioned. The Bolivian Institute of Foreign Trade and ANAPO claim that the soy complex generates over 100,000 direct and indirect jobs (IBCE 2014). Over 70,000 of these jobs are classified as "producers"; yet as previously discussed, the vast majority of these "producers" are excluded from the production process. As Suárez, Camburn and Crespo (2010) elaborate, the other direct and indirect employment consists of agricultural commercial stores, internal transportation, storage and processing facilities, transportation for export and seed facilities (see Table 3.2).

While these estimates are used among agro-industry proponents and various state actors to justify the continued development and expansion of the soy complex, the claim of generating 100,000 jobs is misleading. Aside from the exaggeration of direct employment, the other significant employment claims in storage (1,431) and transportation (26,824) involve temporary and precarious jobs. In my research I found that many of the storage and processing facilities employ two to six full-time staff, seven to fourteen part-time technicians and another seven to fourteen part-time general labourers. Further, the transport truck drivers (internal) are hired during harvest, which spans only a few months of the year and does not offer any type of job security or benefits. Finally, the job numbers provided by ANAPO are for the soybean summer harvest — the busiest and most lucrative time of the year for agricultural production. For winter harvests, the estimates for total employment drop to just over 40,000 and include the same part-time and precarious jobs. Measurements of the employment generation of an industry should consist of stable, annual employment, not precarious one- to two-month seasonal labour opportunities.

Gender and Generational Forms of Exclusion

For the rural youth — the children of Andean colonist farmers — opportunities for employment are few. In the context of soybean farming, a small plot of 50 hectares or less is insufficient if divided between siblings, making it necessary to acquire more land or find employment elsewhere. The lack of industrialization and secure and stable employment opportunities affiliated with the soy complex is problematic, as rural youth are pressured to find employment in urban centres with no clear pathway or opportunities to do so. This raises questions as to where the rural youth will go and what options are available. In reference to Bernstein's (2004) agrarian question of labour, the soy complex in Bolivia is not capable of generating sufficient or sufficiently secure employment to provide a living wage to the great majority (see Li 2009, 2011). This is particularly problematic for rural youth who are actually eager and interested in becoming farmers in the mechanized agricultural sector in Santa Cruz. They are "confronted by the narrowing and sometimes complete closure of access to land" (White 2012: 12) as well as the high costs of production and a lack of access to machinery, capital and credit.

Alfredo Armellon, leader of the Organization of Young Patriots of Cuatro Cañadas (Organización de Jovenes Patriotas de Cuatro Cañadas, JPCC), told me the rural youth will not back down from their right to a dignified livelihood in their community and to a sustainable and healthy environment in harmony with Mother Earth. These are rights guaranteed to the rural youth (ages 16–28 years) in Law 342, established on February 5, 2013. Through the Plurinational Youth Council (Consejo Plurinacional de la Juventud), youth can participate in the political process at multiple levels of government; propose policies, plans, programs and projects; and evaluate their execution (Article 15, Law 342). Armellon and the JPCC hope to use this new political space in order to open a university in Cuatro Cañadas, promote cultural activities and more economic opportunities in the municipality so the youth can stay in Cuatro Cañadas and help in its development. Armellon said the current situation offers little opportunity for the youth and many are forced to migrate to the city, eroding the very social base of society, as outsiders with little interest in a more robust development process control all the land, exploiting it for its value while destroying the natural environment. For Armellon and the JPCC, using the formal political process and interacting with the state is important, but they are also mobilizing from below.

Armellon joined Bolivia's Landless Peasants' Movement (Movimiento Sin Tierra, MST) in 2008 and has taken part in land occupations on many occasions. However, the influence of agro-industry (Agricultural Chamber of Eastern Bolivia; ANAPO; Santa Cruz Chamber of Industry, Commerce, Services and Tourism; etc.) combined with new and complex state-society relations characterized by populist, pro-Indigenous *originario* peasant discourses and the MAS government "explicitly instructing the MST to stop occupying land" with unfulfilled promises of an agrarian revolution has simultaneously led to less land occupations by the MST and facilitated continued power and control over the land for the landed and agro-industrial elites (Brabazon and Webber 2014: 449). In December 2013, Law 477 Against Land Occupation and Trafficking (*Ley Contra el Avasallamiento y Tráfico de Tierras*) was established, thus outlawing any form of land occupation and trafficking and increasing the legal sentence to three to eight years for those who take part in such an action (Article 8, Law 477). Armellon confirmed that people are now moving north in search of land, to San José, Guarayos, Concepción and San Javier. The youth are not giving up hope just yet, he explained, as they continue mobilizing to force the state to implement the agrarian revolution it promised in 2006. For Armellon, this is a regional problem, and the politics of the process are complicated, as the landed elite and agro-industry remain highly influential. But waiting for the state to take action is not an option — the youth, with other associations, are mobilizing to act and take their land back. With six siblings, Armellon knows that his father's 50 hectares are not enough for everyone and cannot be divided. This is why he is taking action, both through formal political channels with the JPCC and through direct action from below.

For the youth in Cuatro Cañadas, migrating to the city remains a last resort rather than an aspiration. However, the majority of the rural youth are not as actively engaged and enthusiastic as Armellon and must migrate permanently or migrate seasonally or temporarily to the city in order to provide for their own families and extended families. The youth cannot wait for many years to take over the farm, much less if it entails becoming a type of rentier smallholder. If this trajectory continues, the majority of rural youth will likely be forced to migrate elsewhere. This brings us to some fundamental questions posed by Ben White (2012: 16):

> Will young men and women still have the option, and the necessary support, to engage in environmentally sound, small-scale, mixed farming, providing food and other needs for themselves, their own society and others in distant places? Or will they face only the choice to become poorly paid wage workers or contract farmers, in an endless landscape of monocrop food or fuel feedstock plantations, on land which used to belong to their parents, or to move to an uncertain existence in the informal sector of already crowded cities?

In other words, who will own the countryside and what is the fate of future generations in rural areas (White 2020)? Even among the youth, opportunities for employment are by no means equal. Being a woman in a rural community, especially in the agro-industrial expansion zone of Cuatro Cañadas and San Julián, is much more difficult for a variety of reasons. For young rural women, job prospects are much more limited. The agro-industry tends to be much more male-dominated, as it is extremely rare — socially and culturally — for women to operate heavy machinery in the field. In my household survey of over three hundred households, just 14 percent identified a woman as the head of the household and thus the decision-maker. In most instances, these were widowed or single mothers who had stayed in rural areas. Through participant observation it was also clear that women, for the most part, do not engage in mechanized production in Cuatro Cañadas and San Julián. This gendered social construction that women cannot or should not use heavy machinery has been reinforced by women's predominant role in the unpaid domestic labour market outside of the formal economy, where they are in charge of important components for social reproduction such as child care, meal preparation and cooking, household work and elderly care, among many other tasks. Though this unpaid labour is equally or more important than operating heavy machinery in the field, it is the men who assume the wage-receiving productive activity in the formal economy, giving them more power in the household and the community in general. Importantly, for married couples, private property is now titled in the name of both the husband and wife, but this does not equate to real changes in intrahousehold social relations. Men, as my survey indicates, are still the predominant decision-makers, but we cannot assume that all members of the household necessarily have the same interests (see

White 1986; Razavi 2009). Furthermore, for those smallholders who have access to machinery and actually put their land into production, it is the male youth who engage in such productive activity. Women are rarely considered to inherit the property and are expected to marry young and move to their husband's property to work in the unpaid domestic labour market for social reproduction.

Operating heavy machinery is not the only form of employment from which women are excluded; they also face obstacles as agricultural engineers and agronomists. These types of extension services, which are growing in the community, require engineers to travel alone during the week, visiting farmers in very isolated areas in the countryside. According to agricultural engineers working in and around Cuatro Cañadas and San Julián, as well as young rural women, these jobs tend to be more male-dominated for two main reasons. First, due to the patriarchal structure of gender relations, known as *machismo*, heads of farming households — predominantly men — are reluctant to take the advice of women in managing their production. Second, the vast majority of male partners are uncomfortable with their female partner travelling alone, long distances, and visiting male-dominated farms. These gendered issues may be overlooked or seem insignificant to some, but they have very significant implications for women, especially the youth, living in these areas.

Like the rural youth, women are not passive actors in this story. The leader of the Women's Federation for Intercultural Agricultural Producers of Cuatro Cañadas (Federación de Mujeres Interculturales Productores Agropecuarios Cuatro Cañadas), Rosa Vargas, continues to work with women in the community to implement projects directly targeted for women. Rosa is a widow with 10 hectares of land — seven of which are rented in a *partida* arrangement for soybean production and three of which are unsuitable and fallow lands, she told me. She has three children, who have already migrated elsewhere due to the lack of opportunities in the region. For her, the greatest challenge in the community now is finding opportunities for employment. This is why she initiated the women's federation, which helps support women with productive activities and increase their participation in the economic, social and political issues in the community. Along with twenty other women, she is currently involved in a chicken coop cooperative, which has roughly six thousand chickens. Rosa's vision is to create more opportunities for women to earn their own income since agricultural production has become highly mechanized and there is no available land left in or near the community. Her plans include projects that enable the community to benefit from processing their raw materials, such as chickens and soybeans, so they can sell these consumer products within the community and create more employment.

While these small projects can provide women with income-generating opportunities, they can also be fraught with their own internal tensions. Another prominent woman smallholder, Mrs. Choque, told me that women's organizations are broken, divided and unorganized. Fanny Pisaro, the leader of another village-based women's organization in San Miguel de los Angeles, also expressed her doubts. She participated in a women's chicken coop cooperative but said 50 percent of the members dropped out due to the bureaucracy to get project funding, the time and investment and the little revenue they have received to date. However, the larger issue here is that women are excluded from the soy complex, forced to find other innovative ways to generate income in the productive economy and continue to work as unpaid domestic labourers in the sphere of social reproduction. Even within the processes of productive exclusion and the new forms of land-based resource control, women are faced with deeper levels of exclusion within the household and class relations. Delving more deeply into the intersectionalities of class, gender, generation and ethnicity goes beyond the scope of this book, but are nonetheless important issues to consider in the political economy of agrarian change.

Toxicity and Health Hazards

Aside from the exclusiveness, precariousness and lack of employment generated by the soy complex, the nature of working with and consuming the agro-chemicals associated with GM seeds is also highly dangerous for public health. The majority of farmers, especially smaller-scale farmers and rural wage labourers, mix the agro-chemicals by hand and are further exposed to the chemical substances during spraying, cleaning and disposing of containers. Long-term exposure to these chemical substances is highly dangerous, and they should be handled with safety equipment (including gloves, proper mixing equipment, dust masks, goggles), which is extremely rare in the two central communities in Santa Cruz's soybean expansion zone, Cuatro Cañadas and San Julián.

The main agro-chemicals used in Bolivia are glyphosate, 2,4-D, atrazine and paraquat — all of which are highly controversial due to their high levels of toxicity and association with neurological and reproductive disorders (Catacora-Vargas et al. 2012). Paraquat, for example, has been linked to Parkinson's disease (Tanner et al. 2011; Kamel 2013), while atrazine has been linked to reproductive disorders (Tillitt et al. 2010; Hayes et al. 2011). Glyphosate, the active ingredient in Monsanto's (Bayer's) Roundup Ready herbicide, was recently evaluated by the World Health Organization's International Agency for Research on Cancer, which classified the most heavily used chemical in the soybean sector as "probably carcinogenic to humans," meaning that there is "sufficient evidence of carcinogenicity in experimental animals" and a positive association between exposure to the agent and cancer in humans, though other explanations cannot be completely ruled out (IARC 2015; Guyton et al. 2015). Atrazine and paraquat have been banned in the European Union, while glyphosate has been banned in a few countries but remains controversially legal in the EU.

Data shared with me from the Bolivian Ministry of Health reveals that the incidence of agro-chemical poisoning in Santa Cruz increased from 183 cases in 2010 to 475 in 2015, which is an average of almost one per day over the past five years. Health workers and hospital staff in Cuatro Cañadas and San Julián contend that while they do not have long-term data on cancer rates, common health problems increasing in the community that are associated with the use of agro-chemicals include skin disease, gastrointestinal disorders and neurological problems (e.g., dizziness, headaches). While farmers have expressed concerns over newly developed health problems (e.g., skin irritation, headaches), the long-term effects and broader health impacts for the community at large are still unknown.

The extractive character of Bolivia's soy complex is reducing labour opportunities and worsening conditions. The soy complex is particularly discriminatory towards youth seeking to remain in their communities, women looking for jobs in the sector and more generally those with limited access to capital, land or both. The lack of forward and backward linkages produced within Bolivia to create value-added productive opportunities limits employment associated with the soy complex. Instead, processes of productive exclusion, youth and gender discrimination and health threats for producers and consumers characterize the labour conditions of the soy complex.

The Simple Reproduction Squeeze and Surplus Populations

Although many small-scale farmers have maintained their formal rights over their original landholdings, they are increasingly squeezed by new commodity forms of productive relations. Land has become increasingly scarce and expensive, labour almost obsolete and means of production (GM seeds, agro-chemical inputs, machinery) appropriated by industry. Small-scale landholders are experiencing a "simple reproduction squeeze," which excludes them from reproducing themselves as farmers, yet does not provide opportunities to transition into wage labourers (Bernstein 1979: 427). The rural majority residing in Bolivia's soybean expansion zone could very well be subject to what Tania Li (2009) refers to as surplus populations. Li distinguishes this concept from Marx's relative surplus population, which becomes part of a reserve army of labour serving to keep wages low for increased capital accumulation. In Li's (2009: 69) formulation, however, she points to new dynamics in which "places (or their resources) are useful, but the people are not, so that dispossession is detached from any prospect of labour absorption." In Bolivia's soybean expansion zone, dispossession is occurring through productive exclusion as capital-poor farmers lack access mechanisms to put their land into production. As Li (2009: 68) states, "The key to [people's] predicament is that their labour is surplus *in relation* to its utility for capital." Labour is no longer sought after in Bolivia's soybean expansion zone, and the lack of forward and backward linkages within the Bolivian economy is not promising for future labour prospects.

It is in response to this crisis of unemployment that Rosa Vargas and the Women's Federation hope to help and support women with productive activities. Vargas said the biggest challenge in the community now is finding opportunities for employment. The Women's Federation she represents is attempting to do exactly that, "so women and families do not have to leave the community." If families want to stay, she said, they have to find alternative ways to make a living since soybean production provides very few jobs. The lack of job opportunities is felt by many, especially the youth and women. Madelaine, a 23-year-old woman from Cuatro Cañadas, told me that since the expansion of soybeans, there are fewer jobs for those who are not working directly as producers and do not have land. For her and her family, there is less work because everything is mechanized and requires less labour, while new opportunities are non-existent. According to Madelaine, the expansion of soybeans has brought benefits only to those producing; for others, like herself, it has brought negative impacts. There is less work, land is scarcer and more expensive and people are trying to force them off their land. Anthony, a recent high school graduate, is in a similar situation. He said there is no land available for him, and the vast majority (an estimated 80 percent) of his schoolmates are in a similar position. He works for Mennonites as a labourer from time to time, but said there is not much opportunity for the youth since labour opportunities are scarce and land too expensive.

Overall employment in agricultural activities decreased from 37 percent in 2000 to 26 percent in 2009 (INE 2012b). The percentage of the population working in extractive industries, construction and industrial manufacturing also dropped slightly from 17.2 percent to just under 17 percent during the same period, while the percentage of unskilled workers increased 4 percent and the precarious workforce with no benefits or stability continues to grow (INE 2012b). According to the Centre for Labour and Agrarian Development Studies (Centro de Estudios para el Desarrollo Laboral y Agrario), the relative surplus value appropriated by workers, in relation to private capital and the state, has decreased from 34.5 percent in 2003 to 25.6 percent in 2013, while the state's share has almost doubled from 13.6 percent to 26 percent and private capital's share has slightly increased from 52.2 percent to 52.8 percent (CEDLA 2016: 7). In other words, labour exploitation has increased vis-à-vis the state and classes of capital, who now appropriate nearly 75 percent of surplus value production according to my data. The persistence of an economy characterized by extractive enclaves, including the agricultural sector, leaves few prospects for rural youth. What will happen to rural youth in Cuatro Cañadas and San Julián once they are squeezed out by an expanding soy complex? Whether they become absorbed into urban economies or become surplus populations of no utility for capital accumulation remains to be seen.

Yet, while this agrarian transition continues to exclude capital-poor farmers, organized forms of resistance opposing the process are relatively weak. As semiproletarian and petty bourgeois rentiers, smallholders are caught in contradictory class positions, which hinders resistance. Since many have maintained formal ownership over their land (though are subordinated via access and control relations) and receive the large majority of their income through land rent, they do not identify with the proletariat. However, their lack of control over physical capital and continual dependence on land rents do not parallel the interests of the petty bourgeoisie and many still self-identify as peasants (*campesinos*). Many smallholders thus find themselves located between particular class relations and unable to organize as a "class for itself" as their diversified income strategies intersect with their individual histories and identities.

The MST is mostly absent in this region and has largely been incapacitated by the current government's policies against land occupations. Law 477, for example, prohibits land occupations — the MST's primary strategy of resistance and defence of territory — and incarcerates those who illegally occupy lands for three to eight years (UNIR y TIERRA 2014). In Cuatro Cañadas, many small farmers have voiced their frustrations with organizing efforts in the community to make demands to the state or resist the terms of their insertion into the soy complex. According to several small but prominent farmers in the community, the distinct histories, identities and resultant demands and expectations of the very diverse group of small farmers has created difficulties for organizing and alliance building among the *colonizadores* (settlers). The mix of geographical origins, personal experiences and histories and, to a smaller extent, ethnicities has resulted in many barriers to proactively organizing and acting as a "class for itself." As Betty Rueda, former president of the Women's Organization of Cuatro Cañadas (Organización de Mujeres de Cuatro Cañadas), put it to me:

> One of the biggest challenges of the community is unification; everyone migrated to these communities from all over Bolivia and therefore have different mindsets, perspectives and norms. It's hard to organize, unify around a cause and make things happen because people don't see eye to eye on many issues, they have different ideas, values and so on.

Further, the penetration of capital into the countryside has not affected everyone equally or evenly — and since many have retained access to their small landholding plots, there is no desire to join a landless workers' movement.

According to Roberto Churata of CAPPO, the general acquiescence among the *colonizadores* is their loyalty to MAS. After decades of dictatorships and unfavourable neoliberal states, Evo Morales and MAS symbolically and discursively represent their interests. Churata explained to me that many smallholders migrated from cities that are MAS strongholds — Cochabamba, Potosí, Sucre, Oruro — and became part of the struggle to bring Morales and MAS to power. "Their blind faith is fuelled by Indigenous and pro-peasant discourses that favour their interests," he said.

For Alcides Vadillo, former director of INRA and now director of Fundación TIERRA in Santa Cruz, social movements have lost their independence and ability to mobilize to make demands against the state — they have become co-opted. Mrs. Choque, a *colonizadora,* smallholder and shopkeeper who arrived to Cuatro Cañadas in 1992, had a similar perspective. She claimed that the small farmer and peasant associations are corrupt, "the *dirigentes* [leaders] and people at the top of the associations are the only ones who benefit and the rest of the population is left with nothing." Mrs. Choque explained that soybean production has changed the community's social cohesion. "The community has become individualistic. Without unity we cannot advance together," she said.

Without organization and resistance from social movements or the state, the soy complex continues to develop and extend its reach in the

Bolivian lowlands as control over the country's fourth-largest export becomes increasingly concentrated in the hands of a few. Such particular class relations have enabled a state-capital alliance to persist by means of a functional dualism between class fractions of capital and labour, facilitating MAS's control over state power and agro-capitalist elites' control over the soy complex (de Janvry 1981).

Functional Dualism and the State-Society-Capital Nexus

Functional Dualism

The coexistence of capitalist and subsistence agriculture represents what de Janvry (1981) calls functional dualism, in which expanded accumulation is made possible by the downward pressure on wages through the presence of semiproletarians. Since labour is not fully proletarianized, subsistence needs are partially derived from their own production, which permits capitalists to reduce wages to a level below the minimum requirement to maintain and reproduce a fully proletarianized labour force. As Kay (2006: 472) puts it:

> Semi-proletarianization is the only option open to those peasants who wish to retain access to land for reasons of security and survival or because they cannot find sufficiently secure employment as wage workers, either in the rural or urban sector, to risk permanent out-migration.

Situated in contradictory class positions, semiproletarianized smallholders have interests as landowners, wage labourers, simple commodity producers and so on and are thus less likely to organize as a "class for itself." This dualism is particularly functional in sectorally and socially disarticulated economies, whereby "forward linkages in the production of raw materials (plantation and mining) and backward linkages in industrial production (outward- and inward-oriented) do not exist" and where "the necessary relation between production and consumption capacities does not imply a relationship between return to capital and return to labor" (de Janvry 1981: 33–34). Under disarticulation, market expansion does not originate in rising national wages, but rather in export markets abroad and through rents. From the perspective of capital, labour represents a loss for profits, as it does not contribute to the consumer capacity and domestic market expansion as it would in socially and sectorally articulated economies (de Janvry 1981). While functional dualism facilitates increased capital accumulation, it also "implies the increasing proletarianization and impoverishment of the rural masses" (de Janvry 1981: 85).

In the case of the soy complex in Bolivia, wage labour on the farm is almost obsolete, forcing smallholders to find non-farm rural employment or become innovative entrepreneurs through cooperative project initiatives. In contrast to de Janvry's (1981) original conceptualization of functional dualism, the Bolivian context is characterized by the coexistence of capitalist agriculture and smallholder rentiers, whose subsistence needs are not primarily derived from their own production but from the appropriation of rent via *partida* arrangements (McKay and Colque 2016). Not fully divorced from the land, smallholders therefore do not become fully proletarianized, yet they lack the necessary access mechanisms to fully benefit from the fruits of their land. With the ubiquitous use of GM seeds and the influx of largely foreign agro-capital, small-scale farmers have been squeezed by rising production costs,[10] the concentration of landownership and the monopolization of the market by agro-industry (McKay 2018).

As landowners, smallholders' economic interests remain aligned with large-scale landowners and agro-industrial elites — that is, for the continued expansion of the agricultural frontier (in hopes of getting access to more land) and increased productivity (yields) and market prices (based on the Chicago Board of Trade). Instead of mobilizing around labour issues or support for small farmers in relation to medium- and large-scale farmers, they have been incorporated into and thus become dependent on the soy complex. This has demobilized key social movements in the region and enabled a state-capital alliance to develop without a serious threat to the state's legitimacy. As farmers remain tied to the land and usually reserve a small portion to partially support household subsistence, they remain dependent on rents and wage labour activities with little opportunity for advancement in the current political economy. MAS, however, justifies the development and expansion of the soy complex with the claim that nearly 80 percent of soy farmers are small scale, which contributes to agricultural sector employment and food security (Vicepresidente 2012; INE 2013; ANAPO 2011).

Since sectoral linkages (upstream and downstream) depend on external markets (importing value-added capitalized goods and exporting semiprocessed or raw soybean) and demand is derived abroad, the soy complex represents a sectorally and socially disarticulated economic enclave. Labour has become surplus to the needs of capital accumulation, and domestic consumption does not contribute to expanding the internal market for capitalist soybean producers, meaning there is no incentive for the industry to increase wages or support labour since it has been reduced to a net loss for capital accumulation. Nonetheless, by collecting rents and engaging in other precarious income-generating activities, small farmers are able to subsist and support the interests of capital due to their contradictory class positioning. This type of functional dualism has enabled a state-capital alliance to emerge without (yet) having to overcome a legitimacy crisis. So long as functional dualism is maintained, the state-capital alliance will be able to pursue capital accumulation interests at the expense of the rural majority.

State-Society-Capital Nexus: Signs of Crisis?

At least five interrelated dynamics of the state-society-capital nexus enabled MAS to gain and maintain state power by appeasing classes of labour and capital without entering a legitimacy and accumulation crisis: (1) the strong state-society relations that emerged as a result of the Pacto de Unidad both leading up to and after 2006; (2) the inclusion and absorption of key social movement leaders within state institutions; (3) the commodities boom, which allowed state revenues to increase to historic levels and thus increased public investment albeit with a residual approach to poverty reduction; (4) state discourse and identity politics; and (5) functional dualism and social and sectoral disarticulation. Yet many of these factors remain dependent on the extractive sectors and thus highly contingent on commodity prices to fuel the neo-extractivist development model. With the fall in commodities prices and the socioeconomic and ecological crises of soybean production starting to surface,[11] the state-capital alliance has reached a crisis of legitimacy.

In 2012, soybean prices reached a ten-year high at US$623 per ton but then plummeted to around US$250 per ton in 2016 and US$350 per ton in 2018. The economic crisis for producers has been exacerbated by long periods of drought, severely affecting yields and leading to widespread indebtedness. Furthermore, food prices in the soybean expansion zone, including Cuatro Cañadas and San Julián, have increased substantially, especially for basic food staples such as fruit and vegetables. These factors are putting a squeeze on small farmers, who are increasingly opting not to sow the soil in fear of indebtedness. The combination of these economic and ecological crises is likely to force capital-poor small farmers off their land and thus fully proletarianize them, eroding the functional dualism that has partially enabled the state-capital alliance to persist.

But even beyond the soy complex, MAS has jeopardized its relationship with the Pacto de Unidad and the strong state-society relations that brought the party to state power in 2006. The controversial conflict in the Isiboro

Sécure National Park and Indigenous Territory (Territorio Indígena del Parque Nacional Isiboro Sécure, TIPNIS), in which the state authorized the construction of a highway through the TIPNIS Indigenous territory and national park without proper free, prior and informed consent, led to widespread conflict between Indigenous groups and MAS and created tensions among the Pacto de Unidad, eventually leading to a split between its organizational members (see Webber 2015). The administrative capacity of the state and political clientelism was further evident with the 2015 corruption scandal involving the Indigenous Fund (Fondo Indígena), state funding provided to support Indigenous-led development projects. Almost 70 percent of the projects had irregularities with over US$180 million unaccounted for, leading to the prosecution of several Indigenous leaders as well as the resignation of the minister of land and rural development, Nemesia Achacollo (Fundación Pazos Kanki 2016).

To make matters worse, these tensions were intensified by actions taken in response to the fall in commodity prices. With state revenues (and state expenditures) highly dependent on rents from the extractive sector, the fall in commodities prices triggered the need for expanded production to maintain revenues. This prompted the controversial passing of Supreme Decree 2366 in 2015, authorizing hydrocarbon exploration and extraction in existing protected areas, despite declarations by the official ombudsperson (*defensor del pueblo*), Rolando Villena Villegas, that the decree is unconstitutional and violates the rights of Indigenous communities (Defensoría del Pueblo 2016). In addition, the state, along with agro-industrial representatives, announced the expansion of the agricultural frontier from 3 million to 13 million hectares within ten years. Agro-industry is also pushing for the legalization of more GM seeds, including rice, wheat and maize. But this issue has raised concerns among many, particularly the Unified Confederation of Peasants of Bolivia and the rest of the Pacto de Unidad, who organized collectively during the 2015 Agricultural Summit (Cumbre Agraria) to stop the attempt to legalize these GM varieties. Further, the leadership of the Unified Confederation of Peasants of Bolivia publicly announced that they did not support MAS's attempt to change the constitution in order to stay in power for another term. This perhaps surprising move signals the confederation's increased relative autonomy or political positioning and deteriorating relations with MAS in their quest for state power. The fall in commodities prices and the necessity to maintain accumulation interests by means of increased geographical expansion has threatened the state's legitimacy and fractured the strong state-society relation, revealing a mutually beneficial state-capital relation dependent upon the accumulation of capital and political power.

All of these factors together, including minor political scandals,[12] have begun to unravel the dynamic state-society-capital nexus that has enabled MAS to maintain state power while appeasing both classes of labour and capital through the partial fulfilment of its objective and subjective functions.

Conclusion

Agrarian dynamics in Bolivia's lowlands are undergoing an important transition. This chapter has analyzed the politics of agrarian change since Evo Morales and MAS gained control over the state. As the land market became saturated and means of production commodified, smallholders were increasingly excluded from productive activity but maintained ownership over their parcels. Capital-poor smallholders lack the structural and relational access mechanisms necessary to integrate as producers in the soy complex. As a result, smallholders enter into *partida* arrangements, whereby they rent their land to capital-rich farmers with access to technology, capital, markets and authority. These mechanisms of exclusion have differentiated smallholders into semiproletarians and petty bourgeois rentiers, hindering their ability to organize as a "class for itself" as they transition into contradictory class positions between labour and capital. This chapter revealed how such processes of productive exclusion are unfolding, pointing to a trajectory of agrarian change that will leave the rural majority in very precarious positions with few employment opportunities. Control over the value chain has further enhanced these power dynamics and the ability to appropriate more surplus value from the production process. The next chapter analyzes the agro-industrial value-chain, revealing who controls and appropriates surplus value from the upstream and downstream components of the soy complex.

NOTES

1. Grants 200 bolivianos (US$29) per year to children enrolled in public education through to the sixth grade (Exchange rate 1 USD = 6.86 Bs from <www.xe.com> on January 21, 2017).
2. Grants 1,800 bolivianos (US$258) annually to low-income residents aged 60 and over who receive social security payments and 2,400 bolivianos (US$344) to those without social security.
3. Grants 50 bolivianos (US$7) to uninsured mothers for four prenatal medical visits, 120 bolivianos (US$17) for childbirth and 125 bolivianos (US$18) per medical appointment for up to two years (Weisbrot, Ray and Johnston 2009).
4. Converted to USD at a rate of 1 USD = 6.89 Bs. Original data from source is Bs 40.543 billion in 2005 to Bs 221.181 billion in 2015 (MEFP 2015).

5. The Ministry of Economy and Public Finance uses the following sectorial categorizations: infrastructure, productive, social and multisectorial.
6. I refer here to the structural and relational access mechanisms, such as technology, capital, markets, labour, knowledge, authority, identities and social relations (Ribot and Peluso 2003).
7. Including communitarian properties, TCOs and lands not yet formalized.
8. These recent changes in the relation between small-scale landowners and capitalist farmers are influenced by the Argentinian modality known as *pools de siembra*, where an entrepreneur organizes a production plan, offers investors an implementation strategy and then leases the land (Benchimol 2008).
9. Author's calculation based on data from the Agricultural Chamber of Eastern Bolivia, the Bolivian Institute of Foreign Trade and field notes (2014, 2015).
10. From 2002 to 2014, costs of production for soybean farmers increased from US$263 per hectare to US$475 per hectare, according to my data.
11. See, for example, a recent news article in *Pagina Siete*, titled, "Is our agriculture dying? Pests and low prices threaten production" (Díez 2016). See also McKay and Colque (2016).
12. Such as the infamous affair between President Morales and Gabriela Zapata, former manager of China's CAMC Engineering Company, which received several million-dollar contracts from the Morales administration.

REFERENCES

AEMP. 2013. *Estudio Mercado Del Grano de Soya*. La Paz: Autoridad de Fiscalizacion y Control Social de Empresas.

ANAPO. 2011. *Memoria Anual 2011*. Santa Cruz: ANAPO.

____. 2015. *Memoria Anual 2015*. Santa Cruz: ANAPO.

____. 2016. "Soya Sube de Precio En La Bolsa de Chicago." Santa Cruz: ANAPO.

Arce Catacora, Luis Alberto. 2011. *El Nuevo Modelo Económico, Social, Comunitario y Productivo*. La Paz: MEFP.

____. 2015. *El Modelo Económico Social Comunitario Productivo Boliviano*. La Paz: MEFP.

BCB. 2016. *Administración de Las Reservas Internacionales: Gestión 2015*. La Paz: Banco Central de Bolivia.

Benchimol, P. 2008. "La Concentracion de La Tierra: Latifundios y Pools de Siembra." *Pagina 12*.

Bernstein, Henry. 1979. "African Peasantries: A Theoretical Framework." *Journal of Peasant Studies*, 6, 4: 421–443.

____. 1992. "Poverty and the Poor." In Henry Bernstein, Ben Crow, and Hazel Johnson (eds.), *Rural Livelihoods: Crises and Responses*. Oxford, UK: Oxford University Press.

____. 2004. "'Changing Before Our Very Eyes': Agrarian Questions and the Politics of Land in Capitalism Today." *Journal of Agrarian Change*, 4, 1/2: 190–225.

____. 2009. "V.I. Lenin and A.V. Chayanov: Looking Back, Looking Forward." *Journal of Peasant Studies*, 36, 1: 55–81.

Brabazon, Honor, and Jeffery R. Webber. 2014. "Evo Morales and the MST in Bolivia:

Continuities and Discontinuities in Agrarian Reform." *Journal of Agrarian Change,* 14, 3: 435–465.
Catacora-Vargas, Georgina, Pablo Galeano, Sarah Zanon Agapito-Tenfen, Darìo Aranda, Tomàs Palau, and Rubens Onofre Nodari. 2012. *Soybean Production in the Southern Cone of the Americas : Update on Land and Pesticide Use.* Norway: GenOk — Centre for Biosafety.
CEDLA. 2016. "Diez Años y Bolivia No Cambió." *Alerta Laboral,* no. 76. La Paz: CEDLA.
Clapp, Jennifer. 2014. "Financialization, Distance, and Global Food Politics." *Journal of Peasant Studies,* 41, 5: 797–814.
Clapp, Roger A.J. 1988. "Representing Reciprocity, Reproducing Domination: Ideology and the Labour Process in Latin American Contract Farming." *Journal of Peasant Studies,* 16, 1: 5–39.
Colque, Gonzalo. 2014. *Expansión de la frontera agrícola: Luchas por el control y apropiación de la tierra en el oriente boliviano.* La Paz: TIERRA.
Colque, Gonzalo, Efraín Tinta, and Esteban Sanjinés. 2016. *Segunda Reforma Agraria: Una Historia Que Incomoda.* La Paz: TIERRA.
Cordoba, Diana, and Kees Jansen. 2014. "The Return of the State: Neocollectivism, Agrarian Politics and Images of Technological Progress in the MAS Era in Bolivia." *Journal of Agrarian Change,* 14, 4: 480–500.
de Janvry, Alain. 1981. *The Agrarian Question and Reformism in Latin America.* Baltimore: Johns Hopkins University Press.
Defensoria del Pueblo. 2016. *Sin los Pueblos Indígenas no hay Estado Plurinacional.* La Paz: Defensoria del Pueblo.
Díez, Gabriel L. 2016. "¿El Agro Se Nos Muere? Las Plagas y Los 'Precios Bajos' Amenazan La Producción." *Págine Siete,* May 2.
Fearnside, Philip M. 2001. "Soybean Cultivation as a Threat to the Environment in Brazil." *Environmental Conservation,* 28, 01: 23–38.
Fundacíon Pazos Kanki. 2016. "La verdad sobre el Fondo Indígena: Un modelo 'vivioso' de gestión pública." La Paz: Fundacíon Pazos Kanki.
García Linera, Álvaro. 2012. *Geopolitics of the Amazon.* La Paz: Vicepresidencia Del Estado Plurinacional de Bolivia.
Ghosh, Jayati. 2015. "Emerging Markets and Development: Is There a Contradiction?" In *Malcolm Adisheshaiah Lecture.* Chennai.
Gudynas, Eduardo. 2010. "The New Extractivism of the 21st Century: Ten Urgent Theses about Extractivism in Relation to Current South American Progressivism." *Americas Program Report,* January 21: 1–14.
Guyton, K.Z., D. Loomis, Y. Grosse, F. El Ghissassi, L. Benbrahm-Tallaa, and N. Guha. 2015. "Carcinogenicity of Tetrachlorvinphos, Parathion, Malathion, Diazinon, and Glyphosate." *The Lancet Oncology,* 16, 5: 490–491.
Hayes, T.B., L.L. Anderson, V.R. Beasley, S.R. de Solla, T. Iguchi, and H. Ingraham. 2011. "Demasculinization and Feminization of Male Gonads by Atrazine: Consistent Effects across Vertebrate Classes." *Journal of Steroid Biochemistry and Molecular Biology,* 127, 1–2: 64–73.
IARC (International Agency for Research on Cance). 2015. *Evaluations of Five Organophosphate Insecticides and Herbicides.* Geneva.

IBCE. 2014. *Soya: Su Importancia Como Cadena de Valor Agroproductiva En Bolivia*. Santa Cruz: IBCE.
____. 2016. *Bolivia: Comercio Exterior de Alimentos*. Santa Cruz: IBCE.
INE. 2001. *Resultados Preliminares Censo Nacional de Población Y Vivienda. Bolivia*. La Paz: INE.
____. 2012a. *Ficha Resúmen Censo Pobalción Y Vivienda 2012*. La Paz: INE.
____. 2012b. *Información Estadística*. La Paz: INE.
____. 2013. *Primer Censo Agropecuario*. La Paz: INE.
____. 2015a. *Comercio Exterior*. La Paz: INE.
____. 2015b. *Primer Censo Agropecuario 2013*. La Paz: INE.
____. 2016. "Salario Minimo Nacional." *Información Estadística.*. La Paz: INE.
Kamel, F. 2013. "Paths from Pesticides to Parkinson's." *Science,* 341 (6147): 722–723.
Kay, Cristóbal. 2006. "Rural Poverty and Development Strategies in Latin America." *Journal of Agrarian Change,* 6, 4: 455–508.
Kersson, Tanya. 2013. *Food Sovereignty and the Quinoa Boom in Bolivia*. 79. *Food Sovereignty: A Critical Dialogue*. International Conference. New Haven: Yale University.
Li, Tania Murray. 2009. "To Make Live or Let Die? Rural Dispossession and the Protection of Surplus Populations." *Antipode,* 41, S1: 66–93.
____. 2011. "Centering Labor in the Land Grab Debate." *Journal of Peasant Studies,* 38, 2: 281–298.
McKay, Ben M. 2017. "Agrarian Extractivism in Bolivia." *World Development,* 97: 199–211.
____. 2018. "Control Grabbing and Value-Chain Agriculture: BRICS, MICs and Bolivia's Soy Complex." *Globalizations,* 15, 1: 74–91.
McKay, Ben, and Gonzalo Colque. 2016. "Bolivia's Soy Complex: The Development of 'Productive Exclusion.'" *Journal of Peasant Studies,* 43, 2: 583–610.
McKay, Ben, Ryan Nehring, and Marygold Walsh-Dilley. 2014. "The 'State' of Food Sovereignty in Latin America: Political Projects and Alternative Pathways in Venezuela, Ecuador, and Bolivia." *Journal of Peasant Studies,* 41, 6: 1175–1200.
MEFP (Ministry of Economy and Public Finance). 2015. *Proyecto Presupuesto General Del Estado Gestion 2016*. La Paz: Ministerio de Economía y Finanzas Públicas
O'Connor, James. 1973. *The Fiscal Crisis of the State*. New York: St. Martin's Press.
Quandl. 2016. "Bolivia Total Investment, % of GDP." Quandl.
Quispe, Aline. 2015. "Importación de Alimentos Casi Se Duplica En Los Últimos Cinco Años." *La Razón,* July 19.
Razavi, Shahra. 2009. "Engendering the Political Economy of Agrarian Change." *Journal of Peasant Studies,* 36, 1: 197–226.
Ribot, Jesse C., and Nancy Lee Peluso. 2003. "A Theory of Access." *Rural Sociology,* 68, 2: 153–181.
Suárez, Rosa Virginia, Mark Camburn, and Sara Crespo. 2010. *El Pequeño Productor En El Cluster de La Soya: Caso Cruceño*. Santa Cruz: PROBIOMA.
Tanner, C.M., F. Kamel, G.W. Ross, J.A. Hoppin, S.M. Goldman, and M. Korell. 2011. "Rotenone, Paraquat, and Parkinson's Disease." *Environmental Health Perspectives,* 119: 866–872.
Tillitt, D.E., D.M. Papoulias, J.J. Whyte, and C.A. Richter. 2010. "Atrazine Reduces

Reproduction in Fathead Minnos (Pimephales Promelas)." *Aquatic Toxicology*, 99, 2: 149–159.
UNIR y TIERRA. 2014. DOCE: "Conflictos de tierra y recursos naturales en Bolivia." Boletín. Trimestral, numero 2, agosto–octubre 2014.
Vicepresidente. 2012. "Gobierno y CAO Acuerdan Ampliar La Frontera Agricola Para Garantizar Soberanía Alimentaria." La Paz: *Vicepresidencia Del Estado Plurinacional de Bolivia*.
Watts, Michael J. 1994. "Life under Contract: Contract Farming, Agrarian Restructuring, and Flexible Accumulation." In Peter D. Little and Michael J. Watts (eds.), *Living under Contract: Contract Farming and Agrarian Transformation in Sub-Saharan Africa*. Madison: University of Wisconsin Press.
Webber, Jeffery R. 2011. *From Rebellion to Reform in Bolivia*. Chicago: Haymarket Books.
____. 2015. "Revolution against 'Progress': Neo-Extractivism, the Compensatory State, and the Tipnis Conflict in Bolivia." In Susan J. Spronk and Jeffrey R. Webber (eds.), *Crisis and Contradiction: Marxist Perspectives on Latin America in the Global Political Economy*. Leiden: Brill.
Weisbrot, Mark, Rebecca Ray, and Jake Johnston. 2009. *Bolivia: The Economy During the Morales Administration*. CEPR *Reports and Issue Briefs*. Washington, DC: CEPR.
White, Ben. 2012. "Agriculture and the Generation Problem: Rural Youth, Employment and the Future of Farming." IDS *Bulletin*, 43, 6: 9–19.
____. 2020. *Agriculture and the Generation Problem*. Halifax: Fernwood Publishing.
White, Christine Pelzer. 1986. "Everyday Resistance, Socialist Revolution and Rural Development: The Vietnamese Case." *Journal of Peasant Studies*, 13, 2: 49–63.
World Bank. 2007. *World Development Report 2008: Agriculture for Development. World Development Report 2008*. Washington: World Bank.
____. 2016a. "World DataBank." Washington: World Bank.
____. 2016b. *The Commodity Cycle in Latin America: Mirages and Dilemmas*. Washington: World Bank.

4 Value-Chain Control: Relations of Debt and Dependency

> Before, the agro-chemicals were better; one chemical took care of everything. Now the technological packages require one product for one pest, another for a different pest, another for a weed and so on. Almost every year we have a new type of weed or pest that must be dealt with. Costs are increasing, but our yields are not. The only ones who keep benefitting are the agribusiness companies selling the chemicals.
>
> — *Mr. Fehr, Mennonite farmer who immigrated to Santa Cruz from Mexico in 1983*

This chapter analyzes Bolivia's industrial value-chain agriculture, disaggregating the agro-industrial value chain and revealing where the "value" being generated is appropriated and how the terms of control and access are changing.[1] The legalization of GM soybeans and the resultant appropriationism has opened new spaces for capital accumulation and enabled capital to penetrate, particularly from Brazil, Argentina and China. By examining the upstream and downstream components of the soy complex, this chapter reveals the sectoral disarticulation of agriculture in Bolivia. While the *partida* arrangement has rendered smallholders in contradictory class positions, value-chain agriculture has created new relations of debt and dependency between those who put land into production.

Industrial Value-Chain Agriculture and Transnational Capital

Economic incentives were not the only reason many farmers abandoned diversified crop production for monocultures. Mrs. Choque, for example, arrived to the soy expansion region in the late 1980s. The daughter of a *colonizador* and trade union leader, her family used to produce maize, rice, yucca, plantains, tomatoes, onions and other vegetables; they also had a few heads of cattle and pigs. The only things they needed to buy, she explained, were salt and oil. They worked their land using family labour, mainly producing for household consumption, while selling surplus production in the local markets and engaging in exchange with neighbours. In the early 2000s, the Brazilian agribusiness Sojima, which controls over 100,000 hectares in the region, purchased vast amounts of land near their family's parcel for large-scale GM soybean production. The company uses aircraft fumigation, contaminating the nearby area with agro-chemicals such as glyphosate, 2,4-D, atrazine and paraquat. As the soil of all nearby parcels became contaminated due to aircraft fumigation and run-off, farmers were forced to make the transition to GM (glyphosate resistant) crop production, Mrs. Choque told me. This is a common story not only in her community but throughout the agricultural expansion zone in Santa Cruz.

In her community of Villa Primavera, only two out of twenty families have agricultural machinery. The rest, like herself, engage in a *partida* agreement with someone who has machinery to work their land. Mrs. Choque said that a Brazilian landowner works the majority of the land in the community, and though he does not formally own the land, he has direct access to it and derives the most benefits from it. When asked about the future of small farmers in the region, Mrs. Choque's response was quite grim. "In the future, small farmers are not going to be able to produce." She went on to say,

> Every year the costs of production are increasing, as we need to buy more and more chemicals. The weather has also changed; it is less predictable and we have less rainfall. And since the majority of us [small farmers] don't have access to machinery, we are dependent on others and have to wait until they have time to work our land, losing out on the best times for sowing, fumigating and harvesting.

She explained that in the near future her family plans on transitioning their land back to a diversified production system for self-consumption with a variety of vegetables, cattle and pigs, returning to the peasant way of life that they had before. Though worried about the surrounding contamination of the air, land and water, she was frustrated by not having any control over her land and the production process. For her, this was not farming as she knows it, but an industrial process exploiting the land and people for profits.

While most smallholders have entered into a *partida* arrangement, others have advanced and built up enough savings to buy a tractor and have become fully integrated into the soy complex, dependent on corporate-controlled agro-industrial inputs such as GM seeds and agro-chemicals (i.e., the technological package, complete with growing instructions). Short-term credit and growing contracts have bound farmers into relationships of dependency with agribusiness as they enter into a cycle of indebtedness and control. As McMichael (2013: 671) puts it, "The producer enters a particular kind of value relation that has the potential to become an instrument of control, debt dependency and dispossession." This is precisely the type of value relation that has come to control farmers in Santa Cruz. Farmers' autonomy over their land is threatened, as it becomes nearly impossible to break away from these chains of dependency due to both economic (supplier contracts, indebtedness) and ecological (soil degradation, contamination, large-scale spraying activity) circumstances.

The introduction of GM soybeans has opened up new market opportunities for agribusiness, as Bolivia's untapped agricultural market launched a new frontier of accumulation. Rather than purchasing land, transnational capital can still appropriate value from industrial agriculture via agro-inputs, storage and processing facilities, credit and debt relations and export markets. This is another form of control grabbing in Bolivia's agricultural sector. Four of the top six companies that control 85 percent of the soybean market for storage, processing (silos) and exports are owned by transnational agribusinesses, which include US-based multinationals ADM and Cargill (see McKay 2018; AEMP 2013). With oligopoly control over the soybean market, the top six companies are able to set prices and greatly influence crop production. Through supply contracts, these companies have a high degree of control over the production process, as they demand specific quality standards that require the use of certain inputs and technological packages. They also have access to export markets and therefore control over the gateway through which the country's soybeans realize their value.

Without actually owning the land or having legal land tenure rights, the relations of control and access to land and its productive resources are largely in the hands of agro-industrial capital. Farmers bear the majority of the risk in this value relation. International price volatility, drought, floods, pests and weeds and so on are all potential threats that must be absorbed by the producer. Meanwhile, agribusiness benefits from the sale of agro-inputs — such as seeds, agro-chemicals, machinery, technical assistance, credit — and often binds the buyer of its products (the producer) into selling their crops, in their entirety, back to the corporation's silos and processing facilities. Further, the *partida* arrangement operates within these contract-farming schemes since the capitalized farmers working the lands of non-capitalized farmers have contracts with agro-industrial companies. In other words, while the capitalized farmers appropriate much of the surplus from the non-capitalized smallholders, agribusiness companies appropriate surplus from the producers through contract farming. The value-chain dynamic thus works as a chain of control with subsequent value appropriation along the chain.

The terms of access and control have been transformed. Owning land is no longer a sufficient asset when one enters into this particular type of value relation, becoming dependent on agribusiness both for the necessary factors of production and to sell the final product. McMichael (2013: 672), for example, breaks down the value-chain relation as establishing "chains of dependency, with smallholders entering markets over which they have no ultimate control," while serving to "generate value that can be appropriated by agribusiness and its financiers — in the commodity form of food, feed and agrofuels for elite consumers, redistributing value from producers to corporate financiers (whether in agribusiness or any other economic sector)." All the risks of production are therefore assumed by the producers, while they add value through labour power and the ecological value extracted from their lands.

At the time of harvest, producers sell their crops to the agro-industry, receiving a price per ton that is bound to the Chicago Board of Trade and discounted, on average, US$70 per ton according to the adjustments agreed upon by the six companies that control Bolivia's silo and export markets (FAOSTAT 2016; ANAPO 2016). To clear and prepare the land and make the necessary initial investment for the next season, indebtedness through supplier contracts is usually a necessity. Debt is therefore a key mechanism of control within the value-chain relation, "constituting the 'chain' through which such new contract farming is activated, reproduced and, in some cases, dispossessed" (McMichael 2013: 672). Of course, those with more access to capital, credit, land and machinery have greater control over the production and decision-making process. Approximately one-third of farmers in Cuatro Cañadas and San Julián own a tractor but not other mechanized farm machinery, meaning that they at least need to hire operational services such as harvesting and transportation or enter into a *partida* arrangement to carry out production from seeding to harvest (INE 2015). Relations of value-chain control thus vary, as farmers with different access mechanisms are incorporated accordingly.

While it is possible to quantify the value appropriated (or retained) by smallholders in the *partida* arrangement, given that the terms between smallholders and capitalized producers fluctuate 18 to 25 percent and the costs of production and soybean prices are available, it is much more difficult to quantify the value appropriated by agribusiness companies in contract farming schemes. However, we can determine the concentration of control of the upstream and downstream components of the value chain and the origins of capital and manufacturing. For processors, it is also possible to calculate the crush value of the soybean industry. The soybean crush is the process of converting soybeans into soybean meal and soybean oil, and the relationship between their prices is called the gross processing margin (GPM) (Chicago Board of Trade 2006). The crush spread, or GPM, is a measurement of the profit margin for soybean processors. While many factors affect the soybean crush spread, "soybean prices are typically lowest at harvest and trend higher during the year as storage, interest, and insurance costs accumulate over time," according to a report by the Chicago Board of Trade (2006: 1). This means that producers receive the lowest price for the oilseed grain at harvest, and agribusiness companies who store, process and trade the crop appropriate more value as the price increases along the chain. Soybeans are crushed into meal (73.3 percent), oil (18.3 percent), hulls (6.7 percent) and waste (1.7 percent). The GPM or soybean crush is calculated using a common denominator of US dollar per metric ton and the following equation:

$$\begin{aligned} \text{GPM} \quad = \quad & \text{price of soybean meal (\$403.28)} * 73.3\% \\ & + \text{price of soybean oil (\$669.86)} * 18.3\% \\ & - \text{price of soybeans (\$390.40)} \end{aligned}$$

Based on prices from the Chicago Board of Trade, the soybean crush spread for July 2016 is US$27.79 per metric ton. This means that for every metric ton of soybean produced in Bolivia, agro-industry appropriates US$27.79. In the summer harvest of 2014–15, Bolivia produced 2,106,600 metric tons of soybeans. Assuming a GPM of US$27.79, agro-industry would have appropriated US$58,542,414 from the crush for that harvest alone. Table 4.1 denotes the net revenue gains (or losses) based on data from two periods.[2]

Agro-industry maintains a consistent revenue based on the GPM rather than directly correlated with soybean prices alone. Producers, who are the capitalized farmers working the land of smallholder rentiers, take on most of the risk as they invest in agro-inputs to put land into production, often through debt relations, and are thus subject to price and yield volatility and natural disasters. Smallholder rentiers forfeit the use of their land and may

Table 4.1 Revenue Distribution of the Soy Complex: Smallholder Rentiers and Producers

Net Revenue for Soybean Production, 2016 Prices		
	Smallholder rentier	Producer
Partida contract	25% of net revenue	75% of net revenue
Costs of production (US$ per hectare)	N/A	463.62
Soybean price ($US per ton)	N/A	230
Yield (ton per hectare)	N/A	2
Gross revenue per hectare	N/A	460
Net revenue per hectare	0	−3.62
Net Revenue for Soybean Production, Average Prices from Boom Years (2008–14)		
	Smallholder rentier	Producer
Partida contract	25% of net revenue	75% of net revenue
Costs of production (US$ per hectare)	463.62	463.62
Soybean price (US$ per ton)	338.88	338.88
Yield (ton per hectare)	2	2
Gross revenue per hectare	677.76	677.76
Net revenue per hectare	53.54	160.61

Source: Author's field notes, 2014–15.

benefit minimally (as during the boom years from 2008 to 2014) or may receive nothing (as in 2016) but avoid entering into debt. During boom years, producers did retain significant profits of approximately US$160 per hectare when working the land of smallholders in a *partida* arrangement. When working their own land with access to all means of production (tractor, harvester, fumigator) and thus not incurring costs of operations (machinery rentals), producers retained profits upwards of US$207 per hectare based on 2016 figures and US$425 per hectare during the boom years. This is the ideal type of producer profile that all smallholders aspire to and that pulls farmers into the soy complex. However, those who retain such profits represent between 5 percent and 20 percent of the total population of soybean producers. Most smallholders are increasingly marginalized, forced to sell their labour power because income derived from the *partida* arrangement is uncertain, subject to volatile prices, unpredictable climate conditions and inconsistent yields. Agro-industry, on the other hand, not only appropriates surplus value from the soybean crush but also has transformed natural components of the agricultural production process into industrial activities to be reincorporated as agricultural inputs, appropriating value from these new agro-industrial inputs (Goodman, Sorj and Wilkinson 1987).

In explaining the processes of capital penetration via industrial value-chain agriculture, Goodman, Sorj, and Wilkinson (1987: 8) demonstrate how capital "create[s] sectors of accumulation by re-structuring the inherited 'pre-industrial' rural production process." As capital accumulation is restricted in agricultural production due to inherent natural plant cycles and processes, industrial capital seeks to appropriate any and all factors of production, including seeds, organic inputs, labour and land. This has been accomplished in Bolivia's lowlands with GM seeds, agro-chemicals, agricultural machinery and land markets. At the other end of the value chain, agricultural crops are increasingly being used in multiple ways (food, animal feed, fuel, industrial material) and can be (or thought to be) flexed according to market conditions (Borras et al. 2016). Soybeans, for example, can be used as animal feed, food and oils, biodiesel and a petroleum replacement for manufacturing (Oliveira and Schneider 2016). Through scientific and technological advancement, industrial value-chain agriculture appropriates and substitutes the natural inputs and outputs of farming to render it as industrial as possible and open new frontiers for commodification and capital accumulation.

Appropriationism and the technological packages complete with seeds, agro-chemicals and application instructions have led to increases in both the costs and quantity of inputs used in production. In 2004, for example, Bolivia imported 198 tons of soybean seeds at an average cost of US$301 per ton; in 2012, seed imports amounted to 9,862 tons, an increase of nearly 5,000 percent with an average cost of US$738 per ton (INE 2012; AEMP 2013). During the same period, the soybean cultivation area increased from 852,000 hectares to 1,103,390 hectares, an increase of 29.5 percent. This exponential increase of seed imports, which vastly outpaces area expansion, is largely due to the influx of GM soybean seeds after legalization in 2005. The increase reveals the dependency on seed imports over domestically produced seeds. In 2005, GM seeds from Argentina came to dominate the market, accounting for an average of 99.9 percent of Bolivia's soybean imports from 2005 to 2014 (INIAF 2015). Although this has led to a proliferation of agro-chemical and GM seed distributors, just four companies control 86 percent of Bolivia's GM seed distribution market (INIAF 2015).

Since GM soybean seeds are engineered to tolerate the herbicide glyphosate, it comes as no surprise that a positive correlation exists between the increased use of GM soybean seeds and the increased use of herbicides, not only in Bolivia but throughout Latin America (see Catacora-Vargas et al. 2012). The increased use of glyphosate combined with the adoption of a no-tillage seeding system has resulted in the "appearance of weeds resistant to glyphosate in GM soybean production ... resulting in greater application of complementary herbicides" (Catacora-Vargas et al. 2012: 32). Almost all the farmers I interviewed in Cuatro Cañadas and San Julián acknowledged the presence of new pests and weeds since the introduction of GM seeds.

In San Julián, Marcos Churquina Cabezas, who came to the region from Potosí in 1982 and is the president of the Association of Small Agricultural Producers in the East (Asociación de Pequeños Productores Agropecuarios del Oriente), has a similar assessment of GM seeds and agro-chemical use. "In the 1980s," he told me, "we worked with our own labour, no agro-chemicals, no heavy machinery. Now, there are more pests and bad weeds and you cannot harvest anything without agro-chemicals. Everything has changed." Churquina Cabezas explained that many farmers transitioned to GM soybean production due to contamination caused by fumigator planes, which affected neighbouring land, destroying crops not resistant to glyphosate and other agro-chemicals.

CAPPO's founder, Roberto Churata, also shared his insights regarding GM seeds and agro-chemical inputs for small farmers:

> Many farmers today cannot even name the agro-chemical they used last year, or what pests and weeds are affecting their crops. The separation of their relationship with the land has rendered them more individualistic and yield focused. Of course, many do not know the science behind GM seeds and are not aware that agro-chemicals remain in the soil for many years after application. They are caught up in the vicious circle of dependence on technology, increasing costs and more pests and weeds. But it is almost impossible for them to escape this technological trap since they are thinking on a day-to-day or harvest-to-harvest basis. Questions about sustainability and land for future generations come secondary and will be dealt with down the road.

Churata, who in 2015 was a senior official for the mayor's office in San Julián and also works as a private consultant in rural development, is one of the most important political figures representing the interests of small farmers in Santa Cruz. He remains an important advisor and affiliate of the region's largest associations of small farmers — the Association of Small Agricultural Producers in the East and the Integrated Community Association of Agricultural Producers of Cuatro Cañadas (Asociación Comunitaria Integral de Productores Agropecuarios de Cuatro Cañadas) — with a deep understanding of the politics and socio-economic changes taking place regarding the soy complex.

Another key informant who works as an agricultural engineer and agronomist for ANAPO in San Julián also said that pests and plant diseases are increasing every year, requiring more and more agro-chemicals. This agronomist works with over a thousand farmers in the region, making daily visits to multiple farms each day. Having worked for ANAPO for nearly ten years, he has seen firsthand the changes taking place on the land as pests and weeds that never existed in the region before are suddenly appearing. When asked about the future of smallholders given the current trajectory, his perspective was regrettably grim:

> Small farmers with less than 50 hectares and no or little machinery won't survive in this region; they will eventually be bought out, go into debt and be forced to sell their land. It's difficult to say, but I have seen this process unfold over the past seven years.

The data on agro-chemical imports is also quite telling. According to Bolivia's National Service for Agricultural Health and Food Safety (Servicio Nacional de Sanidad Agropecuaria e Inocuidad Alimentaria), from 2010 to 2014 the quantity of agro-chemicals registered in Bolivia increased from 12.6 million kilograms per litre to 38.3 million kilograms per litre in 2014 — a 204 percent increase — while the area under cultivation increased by just 28 percent (SENASAG 2014; ANAPO 2015). Both quantitative and qualitative data make clear that since the introduction of GM soybean seeds, agro-chemical consumption has increased at rates much higher than cultivation area increases. Such agro-chemicals are imported from companies based in China (48 percent), Argentina (22 percent), Brazil (7 percent) and Paraguay (7 percent), among others (SENASEG 2014).

The six companies that have a monopoly over Bolivia's soybean processing, silos and exports, with a 95 percent market share, are also among the top fifty largest revenue-earning companies in the country. However, their contribution to the country's national tax revenue is much lower than their relative revenue ranking, as seen in Table 4.2. The agricultural sector as a whole only contributed 0.9 percent of the national domestic tax revenue in 2013, meaning that not even the state appropriates much value from industrial value-chain agriculture.

Table 4.2 Agro-Industry: 2013 Market Share, Revenue Ranking and Tax Contribution

Company	Origin of Capital	Principal Export Markets	Revenue Ranking and Market Share	Rank and Contribution to Total National Tax Revenue
Gravetal Bolivia S.A.	Venezuela	Venezuela, Colombia, Peru, Ecuador	16th (31%)	77th (0.1%)
Industrias de Aceite S.A. (FINO)	Peru	Colombia, Peru, Chile	9th (22%)	38th (0.2%)
ADM SAO S.A.	US	Colombia, Peru, Chile, Ecuador	11th (13%)	41th (0.2%)
Cargill Bolivia S.A.	US	Colombia, Peru, Chile, Ecuador, Spain	48th (11%)	Not ranked
Industrias Oleaginosas S.A. (RICO)	Bolivia	Colombia, Peru, Chile	28th (9%)	Not ranked
Granos S.R.L.	Bolivia	Peru	34th (9%)	Not ranked

Source: Impuestos Nacionales 2014; Nueva Economía 2015.

Just two of these six companies are owned and operated by Bolivian capital (Granos, 9 percent; Rico, 9 percent), and only two companies (Rico and FINO) produce value-added consumer products derived from soybeans. FINO, for example, takes advantage of the crop's multiple and flexible uses, producing cooking oils (FINO), margarine butter (Regia and Primor), shortening (Karina and Gordito) and soaps and detergent (Uno, Azo, Oso). The majority (87 percent) of soybeans produced in Bolivia, however, are for export.

While soybean flour and meal can be sold as consumer products mainly for animal feed, soybean oilcake is usually processed (toasted, refined) further into meal. Crude soybean oil is also refined and sold as vegetable oil or biodiesel or included in a variety of consumer products such as margarine, paints, soap and so on. This kind of semiprocessing is the result of the soybean crush and is fully controlled by a market oligopoly, lacking sectoral linkages and value-added processing.

Furthermore, heavy machinery — tractors, fumigators and harvesters — that has replaced manual labour and changed the entire production process with substantial productivity increases is also imported, principally from Brazil (61 percent), the United States (10 percent) and Argentina (9 percent) (INE 2016).

The development of industrial agriculture through value-chain relations opens up new frontiers for capital to circulate and accumulate. But what we see in Bolivia is the importation of agro-inputs (seeds, agro-chemicals, machinery) and the exportation of raw or semiprocessed "agro-outputs" (soybeans and derivatives). With both ends of this value chain largely controlled by foreign capital, the soybean complex in Bolivia essentially extracts ecological value from its fertile lands, while the value-added activity (surplus value generated) is appropriated elsewhere.

Control Grabbing and the Spatio-Temporal Fix

Value-chain agriculture has generated a new phase of control grabbing through particular social relations of production, which enable agro-industrial capital to control land and its productive resources without necessarily having tenure rights to the land. This is due to capital-intensive access mechanisms facilitated by the appropriation and commodification of the means of production and value-chain relations of debt and dependency.

In essence, value-chain agriculture has created a spatio-temporal fix, whereby surplus capital is able to circulate and accumulate, appropriating surplus value and later exported as a raw material for further value-added processing elsewhere. Harvey (2003: 115–116) explains the spatio-temporal fix as "a particular kind of solution to capitalist crises through temporal deferral and geographical expansion" that requires

> the production of space, the organization of wholly new territorial divisions of labour, the opening up of new and cheaper resource complexes, of new regions as dynamic spaces of capital accumulation, and the penetration of pre-existing social formations of capitalist social relations and institutional arrangement ... [which] provide important ways to absorb capital and labour surpluses.

As agro-industrial soybean production developed much earlier in neighbouring Argentina and Brazil — both growing hubs of global (agro-) capital — Bolivia offered a strategic and convenient space to absorb capital surpluses. In the 1990s, for example, when many Brazilians purchased land in Bolivia, the Brazilian land market was becoming saturated and expensive, and newer technologies to allow for expansion into the acidic soil of the Cerrado region were still developing (Marques Gimenez 2010; Urioste 2012). This phase of investment was prompted by the opening up of Bolivia's land markets in Santa Cruz, offering new and cheaper spaces for capital absorption. Medium- and large-scale Brazilian farmers such as Iglenio Klaus and Claudio Batista Vega were among those looking for new "greenfield sites" for expansion. While the resettlement programs funded by the United States Agency for International Development in the 1980s were engineered to provide a fix for labour surpluses after neoliberal policies and the tin price crisis generated widespread employment among miners, the opening up of the fertile lowlands of Santa Cruz in the 1990s absorbed surplus agro-capital, particularly from Brazil and Argentina.

With land markets in Santa Cruz at a point of near saturation and uncertainty, capital has penetrated once again via value-chain technologies, appropriationism and debt relations. It has managed to penetrate peasant farming, transforming peasants into small-scale capitalist producers, semiproletarians, petty bourgeois rentiers and landless labourers. This has drastically changed, and continues to change, the social relations of production, power and property in this region. As Harvey (2003: 116) states, "Such geographical expansions, reorganizations, and reconstructions often threaten, however, the values already fixed in place (embedded in the land) but not yet realized." Instead of producing crops for household and local consumption, producers now purchase increasingly expensive, external agro-inputs controlled and produced by foreign capital and, after adding labour and ecological value, sell this product for export to a market oligopoly controlled by foreign capital. As a spatio-temporal fix for industrial agro-capital, value-chain agriculture "encompasses smallholder farms as 'resource complexes' to absorb and create capital" (McMichael 2013: 674).

Since Bolivia does not have the capacity to absorb the surplus value created, it is used as a space to temporarily absorb capital and add (mainly) ecological value, while China — which imports almost two-thirds of the global soy trade — absorbs (indirectly) the surplus value created on a global scale. This is the temporal aspect of the spatio-temporal fix. Very little of the value-added components of the soy complex are absorbed in Bolivia; capital temporarily penetrates the countryside, circulates through the soil and is exported in its commodity form as a soybean to external markets, where it is further processed and fed into the global grain-feed-meat complex.

Taking a broader perspective on value appropriation, we can observe that China largely benefits from both ends of industrial value-chain agriculture for soybean production. First, as a producer of agro-chemicals — a processed, value-added product exported around the world — and second, as the world's largest importer and processor of soybeans primarily to provide for a growing grain-feed-meat complex. In order to appropriate more value-added economic activity domestically, in 1998 China adopted an import strategy through a differential import tax structure, which encourages whole soybean imports (3 percent import tariff) over soy meal (5 percent) and oil (9 percent) (Lee et al. 2016). This import strategy enables processing to occur within China, facilitating industrial value-added production in-country. Furthermore, since China's "going out" (*zou chuqu*) strategy of investing overseas, its political and economic influence in Bolivia and Latin America more generally has increased substantially, as countries move away from the Washington Consensus to a seemingly less stringent Beijing Consensus. However, it remains doubtful that such South-South relations will lead to any meaningful structural changes in terms of altering Latin America's dependence on exporting raw materials (McKay et al. 2017).

Conclusion

This chapter has attempted to disaggregate Bolivia's value-chain agriculture and demonstrate how a new phase of control grabbing has emerged via the penetration of agro-capital, particularly from Brazil, China and Argentina. This type of control grabbing does not necessarily entail having tenure rights to the land, but rather having control over the land-based resources via a value relation characterized by debt and dependency. This can be conceptualized as a spatio-temporal fix, first by the land market saturation in the south of Brazil, which brought many Brazilian agro-capitalists to Bolivia's lowlands, and second by the commodities boom in the 2000s and the subsequent crises (food prices, financial, climate), which triggered more global investment in land and natural resources. The temporal aspect of the fix is due to the lack of value appropriation and absorption within Bolivia as imported value-added commodities (GM seeds, agro-chemicals, machinery) controlled by a market oligopoly circulate through Bolivian soil and then commodities are exported in semiprocessed form as soybeans and derivatives.

The introduction of GM soybean seeds facilitated a new phase of capital penetration into Bolivian agriculture, as appropriationism and value-chain relations have significantly transformed the social relations of production, reproduction, property and power. Capital overflow from Argentina and Brazil, two of the region's most advanced agro-industrial hubs and largest economies, continues, in different ways, to penetrate new spaces for capital accumulation in Bolivia. China, the world's largest manufacturer, has also penetrated via the new dependency on agro-chemicals.

The scale at which these relations of debt and dependency have developed is very significant, as an estimated 86 percent of small farmers, who represent 78 percent of total soy-producing farm units, do not have access to the machinery necessary for sowing and harvesting (Suárez, Camburn and Crespo 2010: 83). Using this framework, this chapter concludes that control grabbing continues in Bolivia — primarily through new mechanisms of resource control by means of industrial value-chain agriculture relations — appropriating and concentrating value in the hands of transnational corporations. While dominant discourses maintain that this model of rural development is generating employment, contributing to food security and food sovereignty, reducing costs of production and benefitting small-scale farmers, I have argued otherwise. The current trajectory of agrarian change is threatening the ability of small-scale farmers to work their lands, increasing the country's dependency on food imports and thus volatile international markets and leading to the extractive social, economic and environmental dynamics that are analyzed in the next chapter.

NOTES

1. This chapter draws from McKay (2018).
2. Several assumptions are made. First, the hypothetical is based on the *partida* arrangement (25:75), costs of production are based on the average calculated in Chapter 3 (US$463.62 per hectare), soybean prices are based on Bolivian prices in 2016 and the average during the boom years from 2008 to 2014, yields are assumed to be 2 tons per hectare and the GPM is based on Chicago Board of Trade data from July 2016.

REFERENCES

AEMP. 2013. "Estudio Mercado Del Grano de Soya." La Paz: Autoridad de Fiscalizacion y Control Social de Empresas.

ANAPO. 2015. *Memoira Anual 2015*. Santa Cruz: Asociacion de Productores de Oleaginosas y Trigo.

____. 2016. "Soya Sube de Precio En La Bolsa de Chicago." <anapobolivia.org/noticias.php?op=1&tipo=1&id=649>.

Borras, Saturnino M. Jr., Jennifer C. Franco, S. Ryan Isakson, Les Levidow, and Pietje

Vervest. 2016. "The Rise of Flex Crops and Commodities: Implications for Research." *Journal of Peasant Studies*, 43, 1: 93–115.
Catacora-Vargas, Georgina, Pablo Galeano, Sarah Zanon Agapito-Tenfen, Darìo Aranda, Tomàs Palau, and Rubens Onofre Nodari. 2012. *Soybean Production in the Southern Cone of the Americas: Update on Land and Pesticide Use*. <genok.com/wp-content/uploads//2013/03/Soybean-Production-in-the-Southern-Cone-of-the-Americas-Update-on-Land-and-Pesticide-Use.pdf>
Chicago Board of Trade. 2006. "CBOT Soybean Crush." Chicago: Chicago Board of Trade.
FAOSTAT. 2016. "Food Balance." Rome.
Goodman, David, Bernardo Sorj, and John Wilkinson. 1987. *From Farming to Biotechnology: A Theory of Agro-Industrial Development*. Oxford, UK: Basil Blackwell.
Harvey, David. 2003. *The New Imperialism*. Oxford, UK: Oxford University Press.
Impuestos Nacionales. 2014. "Memoria 2013." *Servicio de Impuestos Nacionales Vol. 1*. La Paz.
INE. 2012. *Información Estadística*. La Paz: INE.
____. 2015. "Primer Censo Agropecuario 2013." La Paz.
____. 2016. "Comercio Exterior." La Paz.
INIAF. 2015. "INIAF Semillas Santa Cruz, Solicitude de Importacion Recepcionadas." Santa Cruz.
Lee, Tani, Ahn Tran, James Hansen, and Mark Ash. 2016. *Major Factors Affecting Global Soybean and Products Trade Projections*. United States Department of Agriculture, Economic Research Service.
Marques Gimenez, Heloisa. 2010. "O Desenvolvimento Da Cadeia Produtiva Da Soja Na Bolívia e a Presença Brasileira: Uma História Comum." Universidade de São Paulo.
McKay, Ben. 2018. "Control Grabbing and Value-Chain Agriculture: BRICS, MICS and Bolivia's Soy Complex." *Globalizations*, 15, 1: 74–91.
McKay, Ben, Alberto Alonso-Fradejas, Zoe Brent, Yunan Xu, and Sérgio Sauer. 2017. "China and Latin America: towards a new consensus of resource control?" *Third World Thematics: A TWQ Journal*, 1, 5: 592–611.
McMichael, Philip. 2013. "Value-Chain Agriculture and Debt Relations: Contradictory Outcomes." *Third World Quarterly*, 34, 4: 671–690.
Nueva Economía. 2015. "Las 100 Empresas de Bolivia Con Más Ingresos El 2014." Santa Cruz.
Oliveira, Gustavo de L.T., and Mindi Schneider. 2016. "The Politics of Flexing Soybeans: China, Brazil and Global Agroindustrial Restructuring." *Journal of Peasant Studies*, 43, 1: 167–194.
SENASAG. 2014. "Database: Servicio Nacional de Sanidad Agropecuaria e Inocuidad Alimentaria."
Suárez, Rosa Virginia, Mark Camburn, and Sara Crespo. 2010. "El Pequeño Productor En El Cluster de La Soya: Caso Cruceño." Santa Cruz: PROBIOMA.
Urioste, Miguel. 2012. "Concentration and 'Foreignisation' of Land in Bolivia." *Canadian Journal of Development Studies/Revue Canadienne d'études du Développement*, 33, 4: 439–457.

5 Agrarian Extractivism and the Politics of Control

> [The new extractivism is] the only technical means [we have] to distribute the material wealth ... and to allow us to have the material, technical and cognitive conditions to transform its technical and productive base. [Bolivia's extractivist project] is not a goal in itself, but can be the starting point for overcoming extractivism itself.
>
> — *Álvaro García Linera (2012: 33–34), former vice president of Bolivia*

So far, this book has examined some of the complexities of agrarian change in Bolivia with regards to (1) the agro-industrial soy complex in Latin America; (2) the development of Bolivia's agrarian structure in historical context, from revolution and dictatorships to democracy and reform; (3) the rise of Evo Morales and MAS and the agrarian to productive revolution characterized by processes of productive exclusion and functional dualism in the countryside; and (4) the new forms of capital penetration and control via value-chain relations of debt and dependency. In this chapter, these new dynamics of agrarian change are analyzed in the context of the broader neo-extractivist model of development pursued by the MAS government. I argue that agrarian extractivism is a politically and analytically useful concept for understanding these new dynamics and trajectories of agrarian change, because it reveals the very extractive character of capitalist agriculture, particularly in the context of contemporary land-grabbing, flex crops and the increasingly corporatized agro-food system. Agrarian extractivism is not used synonymously with all types of industrial capitalist agriculture, nor is it only in reference to soybean production. It characterizes the very extractive dimensions of certain types of so-called industrial agriculture, which have developed unevenly around the world.

It seeks to challenge legitimating claims used by state and corporate actors that industrial capitalist agriculture fosters inclusive growth, generates employment and contributes to food security.

Extractivism, Neo-Extractivism and Agrarian Extractivism

Extractivism

By means of both colonial coercion and post-colonial "consent" via political-economic institutional arrangements, extractivism has broadly characterized the relationship between the industrialized North and developing South — that is, the exploitation, control and export of raw materials from the latter to fuel the industrial development of the former. Natural resource extraction has generally come to plague the industrial development of raw material export economies by means of economic distortions such as the Dutch disease and the natural resource curse. Indeed, extractivism has been central to Latin American theories of development and underdevelopment from import-substitution industrialization to export-oriented development strategies (see Kay 1989).

Extractivism is by no means a new or novel concept. It broadly refers to "those activities which remove large quantities of natural resources that are not processed (or processed only to a limited degree), especially for export" (Acosta 2013: 62). To be more precise, Gudynas (2013) classifies extractivism, or *extractivismo*, based on three dimensions: (1) high volumes of resources extracted, (2) high intensity of environmental impacts and (3) resources destined for export with little or no processing. Rather than measuring extractivism by the weight of the raw material (in tons, bushels, cubic metres or barrels), Gudynas argues for accounting methods that include material and energy flow analysis such as material inputs per unit of service and the ecological rucksack (see Schmidt-Bleek 1999). This definition distinguishes extractivism from other forms of natural resource appropriation by its high intensity of environmental impacts — toxification, contamination, pollution, soil degradation, deforestation and so on. Finally, extractivism includes only those resources that are exported as raw material or partially processed (Gudynas 2013). As such, extractivism is not synonymous with mining or agricultural production, and has distinct characteristics in terms of quantity, intensity, processing and destination. Furthermore, Acosta's notion of extractivism as a "mode of accumulation" entails "the deep structural logic of production, distribution, exchange, and accumulation" (Chase-Dunn and Hall 2000: 86) and is therefore not simply a technical system of processing nature *through* labour, as suggested by García Linera (2013). Similarly, Gudynas (2015: 189), building off Bunker's (1984) notion of modes of extraction, introduces the concept of modes of appropriation, which describes the different ways of organizing the appropriation of distinct natural resources in specific social and environment contexts. García Linera (2012: 32) conceptualizes extractivism "as the activity that simply extracts raw materials (renewables or non-renewables)" and therefore does not distinguish between the small-scale pluri-activity of Indigenous populations living in protected areas in Brazil known as extractive reserves (*Reserva Extrativista*; see Fearnside 1989) and open-pit mining in Potosí or monocrop soybean production in Santa Cruz.

In the current phase of global capitalism guided by neoliberal economic principles of deregulation, trade liberalization and privatization, multinational corporations have come to monopolize extractive industries worldwide — whether mineral, hydrocarbon or agrarian — continuing a mode of accumulation and appropriation that resembles that of the colonial era. During the 1980s and 1990s, extractivism in Latin America was characterized by a limited state role, the liberalization of capital flows and flexible labour and environmental and territorial regulations (Gudynas 2010a). Whether foreign or domestic capital, investment in extractive sectors has rarely been effective at building forward and backward linkages for productive integration with other complementary sectors. As Acosta (2013: 67) puts it, "An additional classical characteristic of these primary production exporting economies ... is that they are enclaves: the oil sector or the mining sector, as well as many export-oriented farming, forestry or fishing activities, are usually isolated from the rest of the economy." This is largely due to the fact that transnational corporations have come to dominate extractivist projects, bringing much-needed capital investment and technology to capital-poor but resource-rich areas but with little interest in building linkages with other sectors of the domestic economy since the extractivist mode of accumulation and appropriation is fuelled by external markets in the North and emerging economies such as China and India. Extractivism is characterized by social and sectoral disarticulation from the rest of the economy, meaning that the capacity to consume is developed externally (demand for exports) and thus not dependent on a robust internal market or domestic demand (de Janvry 1981).

But after decades of resource and labour exploitation and continued impoverishment, social movements and a political left swept through Latin America at the beginning of the twenty-first century, promising redistributive reforms and a break with the logic of the neoliberal Washington Consensus. With an increased state role and variegated degrees of challenge to neoliberal policies, a new type of extractivist project has emerged, labelled as new extractivism or neo-extractivism.

New or Neo-Extractivism

The new extractivism refers to the increased role of the state in extractive sectors through the nationalization of key industries, public-private partnerships and improved collection of royalties and taxes in order to fund social programs and "ensure a more equitable sharing of the resource wealth" (Veltmeyer 2013: 82). With a particularly Latin American focus, new extractivism has sparked debates among many scholars as to whether it represents a break with conventional extractivist projects, altering exploitative relations of production, or maintains a similar productive and exploitative logic, whereby the state funnels resources to the poor in a residual way in order to maintain legitimacy (Acosta 2013; Bebbington 2009; Bebbington and Humphreys Bebbington 2011; Gudynas 2009, 2013, 2015; Seoane, Taddei and Algranati 2013; Svampa 2013; Veltmeyer 2013; Veltmeyer and Petras 2014; Arsel et al. 2014; Arsel 2012). Rather than the continued dependence on the export of raw materials by transnational corporations, the increased role of the state in extractive sectors was, and continues to be, promoted by progressive left governments in Latin America as a means to reclaim sovereignty over the country's resources, redistribute the rents in the form of social policies and initiate a process of value-added industrialization.

Of course, the Latin American left is not a homogeneous entity, and these new extractivist dynamics play out differently in specific contexts, as can be said with conventional extractivist projects. However, the consensus among leading researchers and scholars is that the new extractivism has not only continued resource extraction under a productive and exploitative logic similar to their predecessors' but is also characterized by increased expansion into new frontiers and greenfield sites, justified with popular discourses of social welfare. As Eduardo Gudynas (2010a: 2), who is credited with coining the term "neo-extractivism," points out:

> This [the promotion of new extractive sectors] is the case with mining in Correa's administration in Ecuador, the support of new iron and lithium mining in Bolivia, the strong state advocacy in promoting the growth of mining in Brazil and Argentina, and, at the same time, the Uruguayan Left participates in prospecting for oil off its coast.

For Gudynas, the new extractivism has become, in large part, a component of the new Latin American left project, based on a logic of accumulation and modernization similar to the neoliberal and neoclassical approaches, whereby the state "end[s] up reproducing the same productive processes, similar relations of power, and the same social and environmental impacts" (Gudynas 2010a: 12).

Bebbington and Humphreys Bebbington (2011: 141–142) find that the underlying logics and socioenvironmental consequences of extractivist projects in neoliberal states such as Peru and so-called post-neoliberal states such as Bolivia and Ecuador "seem very similar regardless of the political project or ideological model." Although in Bolivia and Ecuador the constitutions have been rewritten to grant different forms of autonomy, territory and benefits from the extraction of resources to Indigenous Peoples, Bebbington and Humphreys Bebbington (2011: 140) observe that

> Peru, Ecuador and Bolivia also share a growing intolerance of resistance to this policy and each have greeted this intolerance with increasingly harsh rhetoric, criminalisation of protest (or at least threats to this effect), and a tendency on the part of their executive branches to emit proposals for legislative reform that reduce the scope for the exercise of citizen voice during the project cycle of extractive investment.

Veltmeyer (2016: 778) reaches similar conclusions about Latin America, maintaining that "the left-leaning progressive regimes in the region find themselves entangled in a maze of renewed dependence on natural resource extraction (the 'new extractivism') and primary commodity exports ('reprimarization')." For Veltmeyer, this type of "inclusionary state activism" remains reliant on neoliberal macroeconomic policy and suffers from the inherent contradictions of extractive capitalism (between labour and capital, nature and economic development, and the North and South), which leads to increased inequalities, environmental destruction and a "reprimarization" of the economy (Veltmeyer 2016).

Extractivism has become so central to development policy across the Latin American region that it overrides adverse socioeconomic and environmental concerns, seemingly enjoying a high degree of teleological primacy, or what Arsel, Hogenboom and Pellegrini (2016) describe as the extractive imperative. The extractive imperative goes beyond a set of state policies that facilitate extraction *for* development to extraction becoming a necessary precondition for or even synonymous *with* development. Arsel, Hogenboom and Pellegrini (2016: 881) ground their definition of the the extractive imperative on three ideological positions:

> That intensified extraction is indispensable to advance through a (implicitly Rostowian) process of structural economic transformation; that such a transition away from primary commodity exports to higher value added (and putatively more sustainable) goods and services (biotechnology rather than timber, electric cars rather than lithium ore, etc.) needs to be orchestrated and, to a large extent, executed by the state; and that poverty and inequality need to be addressed urgently throughout this transition and not put aside as the ultimate goal of development.

Extraction, then, becomes imperative for development (understood as advancing through Rostow's stages of economic growth model) when properly and partially controlled by the (developmental) state in order to industrialize and retain value-added surpluses while simultaneously channelling extractive rents to combat poverty and inequality. This is the logic underlying the new extractivism in Latin America and the rationale of Latin America's progressive left governments for pursuing an extractivist development model in the interest of the nation. However, as Arsel, Hogenboom and Pellegrini (2016: 885) point out, this imperative "assumes that a singular, coherent interest of the nation exists" and that the state apparatus is "a Weberian ideal type state that is decisively dominated and operated by efficient bureaucratic machinery." On both counts, it is evident that this is not the case. The extractive imperative has come to serve the interests of the political and economic elites at the cost of severely adverse socioeconomic and environmental implications for the majority. Despite discourses of industrialization, the Bolivian state has failed to facilitate industrial value-added linkages and, although cash transfer programs have led to a decrease in poverty, the lack of structural change concerning productive relations renders marginalized populations vulnerable to shocks such as commodity price volatility, the discontinuity of cash transfers and the uneven distribution of the socioeconomic and environmental costs generated by expanding extractive frontiers.

The New Extractivism in Bolivia

The extractive imperative has become increasingly evident in Bolivia, where legislative reform under Supreme Decree 2366 of May 20, 2015, allows hydrocarbon exploration within protected areas, opening up twenty-two protected areas and roughly 24 million hectares of land for hydrocarbon extraction (Campanini 2015). The new decree is expanding the extractivist frontier for hydrocarbon exploitation, which already compromises eleven out of the country's twenty-two total national protected areas. In terms of land area, 17 percent of land under the National Protected Area System (Sistema Nacional de Áreas Protegidas) are now extractivist zones (Campanini 2015).

Extractivism in Bolivia is indeed part of a broader development plan for industrialization, as stated by García Linera, vice president at the time, during an event held by the United Nations Development Programme for its Human Development Report for Latin America and the Caribbean. He declared that Bolivia will continue to use *extractivismo* for decades to come (Corz 2016). For García Linera, the point of extractivism is to meet the needs of the population, to create wealth with equitable distribution and build upon it a new non-extractive material base to preserve and expand the benefits of the working population (García Linera 2012).

Since 2006, the Bolivian state has increased its share of the domestic economy from 15 percent to 38 percent and now controls some forty-three companies in strategic sectors such as hydrocarbons, telecommunications, electricity, mining, aeronautics and cement (Lazcano 2013; Varela Mendoza 2014). Most notable was the nationalization of the hydrocarbons sector and several adjustments to the mining sector, including the nationalization of the Huanuni mine and favourable policies for mining cooperatives. In 2014, state mining companies represented just 8.7 percent of the total production value, while private mining companies and cooperatives represented 47.4 percent and 43.9 percent, respectively (Fundación Jubileo 2016). Through nationalization of the hydrocarbon sector, the government re-established the country's natural gas as property of the state with non-transferable concessions, bought back shares from companies that had previously taken over state enterprises during the "capitalization" of the 1990s and renegotiated price contracts.

Of most significance, however, was the hydrocarbon law (3058), passed in 2005 during the Carlos Mesa presidency, which increased taxes on hydrocarbon extraction and commercialization from 18 percent to 50 percent and still remains in effect today. In 2014, extractivist rents from the Direct Hydrocarbon Tax (17.5 percent), hydrocarbon royalties (9.8 percent) and mining royalties (1.3 percent) accounted for 28.6 percent of total state revenues from taxes and royalties (Villegas 2015). Tax and royalty increases coincided with a commodities boom and heightened demand, which increased the state's budget some 445 percent — from US$5.9 billion in 2005 to US$32.1 billion in 2015 (MEFP 2015).[1] Despite the increased fiscal capacity of the state, little progress has been made in the way of value-added industrialization, as the country's exports remain dependent on raw materials. From 2006 to 2013, primary product exports, as a share of total exports, increased from 89.4 percent to 96 percent (ECLAC 2014).

García Linera (2012: 32) conceptualizes extractivism as the mere extraction of raw materials and says that "without introducing greater transformation in the work performed, then all societies in the world, capitalist or non-capitalist, are also to a greater or lesser degree extractivist." For García Linera, the central debate rests upon the relations of production when processing nature through labour, yet his analysis disregards extractivism as a mode of accumulation or appropriation, as argued by Acosta (2013) and Gudynas (2015). Acosta and Gudynas of course recognize the literal meaning of the word "extraction," but go beyond the semantics to an analysis of the relations and forms of natural resource extraction in Latin America. García Linera (2012: 34), however, challenges critiques of Bolivia's extractivist development model by first defending extractivism in the simple literal sense of "to pull or draw out" resources, which as a technical system of processing nature through labour has nothing to do with injustices, exploitation or inequality and "can be present in pre-capitalist, capitalist or communitarian societies."

Second, García Linera (2012: 34) and the MAS government defend extractivism on the basis of the very need to "distribute the material wealth generated through extractivism ... to have the material, technical and cognitive conditions to transform its technical and productive base." Opposition to extractivism is labelled as a form of imperialism, or "green imperialism," whereby "the governments of rich nations now use environmental concerns to promote policies that deny underdeveloped nations the right to control and manage their own resources" (Fuentes 2011). This was the strategy used regarding the infamous TIPNIS case, whereby the government defended the construction of a highway through the national park by means of resource nationalism, claiming that rather than violating Indigenous rights and threatening the environment, the highway would secure better access to markets and health services and spur development (Pellegrini 2016). The MAS government, led by one of its leading Marxist scholars, García Linera, has gone on the attack to defend extractivism, claiming that "behind the recently constructed 'extractivist' criticism of the revolutionary and progressive governments, then, lies the shadow of the conservative restoration" (García Linera 2012: 34). In his analysis of the TIPNIS case, García Linera claims that any opposition to the Brazilian-financed TIPNIS highway project, whether intentionally or unintentionally, is counterrevolutionary and defends the interests of the right, who want to keep Bolivia and other developing countries from development and progress. García Linera (2012: 1) writes:

> The tragic course of history so unfolds that the counterrevolution can come hand in hand with a faction of its own builders which, without necessarily advocating it, may as a consequence of the exacerbation of its corporatist, regional or sectoral particularism, and without taking into account the general configuration of overall social forces nationally and internationally, end up defending the interests of the conservative forces of the right and undermining their own revolutionary process. That is precisely what came to happen with the so-called "TIPNIS march."

Extractivism is therefore defended by the state as a form of resource nationalism and as a means to regain its sovereignty from external forces that historically exploited the country's natural resource wealth during the old extractivism of colonial and neoliberal regimes. But as Arsel et al. (2014: 123) argue:

> Nationalization has not resulted in take-over of property rights and the displacement of foreign corporations by economic entities owned or operated by the state, nor even by individuals who are nationals of these countries. Instead, nationalization has left enough space for foreign corporations to enter into various forms of agreements — concessions, joint ventures, etc. — that are blessed by the state.

Those who defend neo-extractivism, such as García Linera and Federico Fuentes (2011), fail to analyze the relations of access and control over the resources being extracted and processed through labour as a technical system. Indeed, as García Linera asserts, it is not the technical form that is the problem, or extractivism per se when defined in a literal sense of drawing out resources. Yet he neglects to analyze the political economy and ecology of extractivism in Bolivia. By ignoring the very modes of accumulation and appropriation, García Linera fails to acknowledge the underlying socioeconomic and environmental implications of extractivism in Bolivia. This is why it is important to deepen our understanding of extractivism, to analyze its characteristics as a mode of accumulation and appropriation, not simply as a technical system or form of production (Acosta 2013; Gudynas 2015).

Agrarian Extractivism

Agriculture is already being included as a form of extractivism in the new or neo-extractivist literature. Gudynas (2010a: 2), for example, has used the term "agricultural extractivism" to refer to agriculture oriented toward monoculture and the use of transgenics, machinery and chemical herbicides with "little or no processing and exportation of the produce as a commodity." Gudynas suggests that this is not an industry and using the term "industry" implies some kind of industrialization or value added — not primary production for export. For Gudynas (2010a; 2010b; 2013), agricultural activity that is characterized by a high volume or intensity of extraction and semiprocessed commodities destined for export is considered extractivism, with particular reference to soybean plantations in Latin America. Giarracca and Teubal (2014: 48) suggest the term "also applies to a certain type of agriculture in which essential resources such as water and fertile land, and biodiversity, are degraded by extractivism." Petras and Veltmeyer (2014: 64) use the term "agro-extractivism" in the context of the agrarian question of the twenty-first century, arguing that what governments such as China and other international investors "primarily seek are lands to meet their security need for agro-food products and energy, while multinational corporations in the extractive sector of the global economy are primarily concerned to feed the lucrative biofuel market by producing oil palm, sugarcane (for ethanol) and soya," or what might be called flex crops. They go on to say that

> agricultural extractivism takes a number of forms, but in the current context that has dominated the debate — apart from the dynamics of land grabbing — has been what we might term the political economy of biofuels capitalism: the conversion of farmland and agriculture for food production into the production of biofuels. (Petras and Veltmeyer 2016: 70)

Maristella Svampa (2013: 118–119) includes agribusiness and biofuels production in her understanding of the new extractivism in Latin America, "due to the fact that they consolidate a model that tends to follow a monoculture, the destruction of biodiversity, a concentration of land ownership and a destructive re-configuration of vast territories" and driven by what she calls the Commodities Consensus, "the beginning of a new economic and political order sustained by the boom in international prices for raw materials and consumer goods, which are increasingly demanded by industrialised and emerging countries" (117).

Agrarian extractivism has therefore been introduced under the umbrella of neo-extractivism to refer broadly to large-scale, intensive monocrop production for export. But what is the extractive character of agrarian extractivism? Are all types of large-scale chemical-intensive monocrop plantations extractive? Evidently, this type of agricultural production can take many forms in terms of land control and use, labour relations, surplus distribution and the social relations of consumption, reproduction and accumulation (Bernstein 2010). Some large-scale plantations may require a large labour force, be cooperatively owned by the workers, reinvest the surplus in the domestic economy creating forward and backward linkages, exploit dynamic intersectoral synergies and produce value-added consumer goods for the domestic market. Yet this type of large-scale industrial agriculture is distinct from that which is highly mechanized and requires minimal wage labour, export oriented with little or no processing, corporate controlled in a monopolized market and highly dependent on external chemical based inputs. Agribusiness or agro-industry may not be inherently extractive as such, which is why it is important to specify the extractive nature of the process.

Agrarian extractivism as conceptualized here builds on much of the aforementioned literature on extractivism, particularly as a mode of accumulation (Acosta 2013) and appropriation (Gudynas 2015), as well as the three dimensions put forth by Gudynas (2013) regarding scale (volume of material extracted), ecological impacts (intensity of extraction) and resource destination (semiprocessed for export). As a mode of accumulation, agrarian extractivism also involves particular social relations of production and reproduction in the current phase of capitalist agriculture in which the surplus value is extracted and labour opportunities and conditions deteriorate via new forms of value-chain control. Taking these factors together with Gudynas's dimensions of extractivism and inspired by the work of Alonso-Fradejas (2015),[2] I characterize agrarian extractivism in Bolivia by the following four interlinked features: (1) significant volumes of extracted materials destined for export with little or no processing, (2) value-chain concentration and sectoral disarticulation, (3) high intensity of environmental degradation and (4) deterioration of labour opportunities and labour conditions in the area or sector. Many of these features have been discussed in the previous chapters and therefore are not discussed in depth in this chapter. These four features are not meant to represent a one-size-fits-all definition for agrarian extractivism; rather, they bring to the fore the extractive character of industrial agriculture across the social, economic and ecological spheres with a particular emphasis on scale (scale of extracted materials and/or scale of capital involved), control (over value chains and control grabbing) and sectoral linkages (or lack thereof) and the extent to which the sector represents an extractive enclave. The degree of extractivism in agrarian sectors will undoubtedly vary in different contexts and crop complexes.[3]

The soy complex should be understood in the context of the broader extractivist-based economy in Bolivia, namely minerals and natural gas, and part of the state's three-pronged extractivist model of development. But while mineral and natural gas extraction contribute significantly to state revenues, the largely foreign-controlled soy complex does not. The increasing role of the state in the Bolivian economy since 2006 has coincided with a somewhat laissez-faire strategy in the agricultural sector. The expansion of the soy complex has also halted the agrarian reform, or agrarian revolution, that was an important part of Morales's political agenda when he came to power in 2006. In the ensuing sections, Bolivia's soy complex is analyzed in terms of the four interlinked features of agrarian extractivism.

Agrarian Extractivism in Bolivia

Significant Volumes of Raw Material Exports

The first dimension of agrarian extractivism as defined here concerns the volume of extracted raw materials destined for export with little or no processing. Volumes are considered large or significant relative to other agricultural-based exports and include the cumulative production of smaller-scale units. Processing is only significant if it generates value-added sectoral linkages and employment opportunities. The area under soybean cultivation has dramatically increased over the past ten years, with the volume of extracted material going from 836,700 metric tons in 2007 to 2,106,600 metric tons in 2014 while land area more than doubled from 428,000 hectares to 935,000 hectares during the same period (ANAPO 2015).[4] In 2013, 2,357,866 metric tons of soybeans and derivatives were destined for export, representing 90 percent of total production (ANAPO 2015; IBCE 2015).

It is the value-added component of the production process that can trigger sectoral articulation, as complementary sectors engage in industrial processing and manufacturing creating employment through intersectoral linkages. When soybeans are semiprocessed into oilcake and meal for export, there is no sectoral articulation and little employment generation. The oilcake must be further processed to be converted into animal feed or consumer products. Relative to Bolivia's agricultural productive capacity, soybean production is significantly high, occupying by far the largest share of acreage under cultivation and generating more export revenues than any other crop. The high volume of soybeans produced, semiprocessed and destined for export represent the first of four features of agrarian extractivism in Bolivia.

Value-Chain Concentration and Sectoral Disarticulation

The second dimension of agrarian extractivism in Bolivia pertains to the concentration of value-chain control and the lack of sectoral articulation. The dynamics of control over each component of the value chain were discussed in depth in Chapter 4. The majority of value-chain components are not produced in Bolivia, meaning their associated surplus value is appropriated elsewhere. Surplus value is produced during the production of these use values, which are imported to Bolivia in order to increase labour productivity and ultimately extract more value from soybean production. The natural fertility of Bolivian soil is a source of use value in the production process, which, through the application of labour power and agro-industrial inputs, produces surplus value represented by the soybean, an agro-commodity exchanged on international markets. Agro-industrial inputs and mechanization have substantially decreased the socially necessary labour time to produce soybeans, reducing the need for labourers and extracting more of nature's use values through intensification, thus increasing the relative surplus value appropriated by agro-industrialists and capitalist producers.

The natural fertility of the soil varies across geographical areas, enabling those who control more favourable soils to appropriate more surplus profit (Marx 1981). The soil's natural fertility increases the productivity of labour and enables the appropriation of surplus profits either by the capitalist producer or by those controlling the land in the form of ground rent (differential rent I) (Marx 1981). Furthermore, different capitals (seeds, agrochemicals, machinery) can also produce more value (at least temporarily, due to decreasing soil fertility) on equal amounts of land using the same amount of labour power. This is the appeal of technological innovation in agriculture, such as high-yielding seed varieties, agro-chemical inputs and advanced mechanization. This is another form of surplus profit extracted from nature (as a use value), which may be appropriated as surplus value by capitalist producers or as ground rent (differential rent II) by landowners (Fine and Saad Filho 2004). In other words, ground rent is the appropriation of surplus profits by landed property. In the context of Bolivia's soy complex, the main source of value is appropriated through ground rent, though some labour is needed to extract the resource and bring it to the market in commodity form.

The most central part of the production of soybeans, which is the basis for the entire complex, is land. Control over the land means control over where the soybean (and surplus value) is produced. The soil and the worker, as Marx (1976: 638) put it, are "the original sources of all wealth." Land serves as the means of production, by providing nutrients for the soybeans to grow, and embodies part of the production process within the soil itself (Harvey 2006). Of course, other necessary inputs, including labour power, seeds and machinery, are required, but land remains central. Yet formal land ownership has become less and less important in appropriating the surplus value from the production process due to processes of productive exclusion and value-chain control.

Bolivia's soy complex can thus be characterized by the importation of finished products (GM seeds, agro-chemicals, machinery), the circulation of this agro-capital through Bolivian soil controlled by a small minority of agro-capitalists, concentrated control of the production process by a few companies and the export of the semiprocessed product. The extraction of the surplus value from the production process and appropriation by a few domestic and multinational companies (value-chain concentration), along with the lack of forward and backward linkages in the domestic economy (sectoral disarticulation), represent a significant dimension of agrarian extractivism in Bolivia.

High Intensity of Environmental Degradation

The third dimension of agrarian extractivism in Bolivia concerns the intensity of environmental degradation in the region. Since this feature has not yet been discussed, I examine it in greater detail than the other features. The intensity of environmental degradation refers to unsustainable farming practices that have lasting effects, most directly on the communities in close proximity to the production process but also beyond. Highly mechanized and GM soybean production is based on a myriad of unsustainable farming and land use practices associated with declining soil fertility and erosion, contamination of water sources, high rates of deforestation and loss of biodiversity, which contribute to climatic changes such as increased flooding and drought (Hecht 2005; Pengue 2005; Müller et al. 2014). This is linked to the heavy use of synthetic fertilizers and agro-chemicals required to treat large-scale monocultures, the mechanization of production and the massive expansion of the agricultural frontier to serve export markets principally for animal feed and biodiesel (Catacora-Vargas et al. 2012). This section focuses on the intensity of environmental degradation faced by rural communities in Santa Cruz with firsthand accounts from smallholders in Cuatro Cañadas and San Julián.

Since the legalization of GM seeds, the quantity of agro-chemicals used in production has far outpaced the cultivation area. Soybean farmers in the expansion zone attest to this, explaining that year after year new types of weeds and pests threaten their crops and require new types of herbicides and pesticides. Personal interviews with farmers in 2014 and 2015 revealed that the majority of small-scale farmers with less than 50 hectares average close to 2 metric tons per hectare of soybean harvest while those medium- and large-scale farmers who possess machinery average closer 3 metric tons per hectare. The lack of machinery, inability to purchase top-quality seed and agro-chemical packages and land quality and location render capital-poor farmers less able to produce and compete and disproportionally harmed both economically and socially from ecological degradation.

Prominent community leader Paulino Sánchez of Nuevo Palmar came to Cuatro Cañadas from Potosí in 1983, receiving 50 hectares from the government. He said that one of the more challenging issues for farmers today is the depletion of the soil's fertility. "The soil is losing its nutrients," he said. "There is compaction from machinery and people use a lot of chemicals, so yields are decreasing." Over the past ten years, yields have fluctuated between 1.3 to 2.7 metric tons per hectare, which is difficult for farmers' economic security since for each hectare, one ton of harvest roughly covers the cost of production, he said. Those who can afford the best seeds and technologies, however, do not suffer the cost of this environmental degradation to the same extent, at least in the immediate term. Sánchez also explained that many people are worried about the risks of investing in production due to high costs and frequent periods of drought and floods. Some people have lost everything due to natural disasters and therefore do not want to risk their entire savings on a tractor or harvester with so much uncertainty. These natural disasters, particularly the effects of El Niño and La Niña, are increasingly affecting not only farmers and their harvests but entire communities. Since 1990, there have been a total of twenty-five floods, which have resulted in the death of 674 people and affected close to three million (EM-DAT 2016). While the expansion of Bolivia's agricultural frontier and the resulting deforestation is certainly not the only cause of the increased frequency and severity of floods and drought, forest loss greatly influences regional and global climates, as forests not only play an important role as a carbon sink but also return water to the atmosphere via the extraction of soil water by tree roots, referred to as "a transpiration service" (Malhi et al. 2008).

A United Nations study reveals that in the past thirty years, Bolivia has lost over 6 million hectares of forest and has one of the highest rates of deforestation per capita in the world (320 square metres per person per year) — twenty times higher than the global average (16 square metres per person per year) (UN-REDD 2010). Seventy-five percent of this deforestation activity is located in Santa Cruz, with an average deforestation rate of 200,000 hectares per year from 2000 to 2010 (Cuéllar et al. 2012).

A study by Müller et al. (2013) found that from 1992 to 2004, 72.6 percent of the 1.88 million hectares of forests cleared in Bolivia's lowlands were remove due to medium- and large-scale mechanized agriculture (53.7 percent) and small-scale agriculture (18.9 percent), with cattle ranching causing the remaining 27.4 percent. This period coincides with the initial expansion of the agricultural frontier when soybean cultivated areas increased from 164,920 hectares in 1992 to 602,000 hectares in 2004 (ANAPO 2015). In the late 1990s, for example, three Mennonite communities abandoned over 100,000 hectares of soybean land due to soil erosion, compaction and exhaustion and moved north to clear new territory, selling their land to cattle ranchers (Fearnside 2001). However, for the period from 2005 to 2010, Müller et al. (2014) found that the principal drivers of deforestation in the lowlands had reversed, with cattle ranching representing 59.7 percent and mechanized agriculture (24.6 percent) and small-scale agriculture (15.9 percent) representing a combined 41.3 percent. As land prices increase and market conditions make growing soybeans more profitable than cattle ranching, agro-industry tends to push cattle ranchers to expand into new areas, triggering more deforestation and opening new areas for future soybean expansion (Fearnside 2001; Hecht 2005; Weis 2013).

Deforestation has not only led to a loss of biodiversity; it also affects the communities that depend on forests for their livelihoods, particularly the Indigenous territories of Lomerío, Guarayos and Isoso, which are located in and around the expanding agricultural frontier. A recent study by Vadillo, Salgado and Muiba (2013) concludes that agro-industrial expansion is one of the major threats to the Indigenous territory of Lomerío and the Chiquitano people, who collectively have the rights to close to 260,000 hectares, 60 percent of which is forest. Guarayos is another Indigenous territory threatened by agro-industrial expansion. Located to the north of the soybean expansion zone, many farmers in Cuatro Cañadas and San Julián are seeking land in and around Guarayos, where the frontier is being extended as a result of illegal deforestation, occupation and illegal land deals between Indigenous leaders and soybean farmers. Despite such threats to Indigenous Peoples and the biodiversity that many depend on for their livelihood, the government's agenda as announced by Vice President García Linera and agro-industrial representatives of the Agricultural Chamber of Eastern Bolivia in 2012 was to increase the agricultural frontier by 1 million hectares per year until 2020 to "guarantee food sovereignty" (Vicepresidente 2012; Heredia Garcia 2014). This exemplifies the state's attempt to justify and legitimize forms of capital accumulation through popular discourses, serving the interests of the landed elites and agro-industrialists while capital-poor farmers and Indigenous Peoples remain excluded and further threatened by the environmental consequences of the expansion.

The dynamics of deforestation run much deeper than the loss of forests and biodiversity. Forests provide important land cover, prevent erosion, absorb rainfall and provide important ecosystem services that regulate weather and climate patterns. There is ample evidence that deforestation amplifies flood risk and exacerbates the severity of El Niño–Southern Oscillation (ENSO) climate cycles (Malhi et al. 2008; Bradshaw et al. 2007). Rapid rates of deforestation have coincided with increased floods in Bolivia, with the most catastrophic floods in recent history in 2007–08 and 2014. In 2007, floods displaced over 100,000 families, killing fifty people and affecting 366,000 hectares of cultivated land, while in 2008, floods resulted in the deaths of another sixty-seven people, displacing ninety-seven families as the river, the Rio Grande, which borders the principal soy-producing communities of El Puente, San Julián, Cuatro Cañadas and Pailon, rose 3 to 4.5 metres (BID 2014). In 2014, eighty-five municipalities were affected, displacing some 24,036 families, destroying 713 homes, killing forty-four people and affecting 352 hectares of cultivated land (BID 2014: 8). In May 2015, over a hundred communities in the municipality of San Julián alone lost much of their harvest due to floods. Abraham Guzman of San Julián lost his entire parcel (45 hectares), while approximately 700 hectares in his community were flooded. For small farmers, this results in almost an entire year's income lost, while their initial investment in agro-inputs leads to indebtedness — sometimes to agro-industry such as ADM, Gravetal, Monica or FINO or to other farmers — which could potentially lead to having to sell their land.

The ENSO phenomenon and floods continue to increase in intensity and frequency. In the 1960s, the department of Santa Cruz experienced normal conditions without the ENSO climate phenomenon 74 percent of the time, while in the first decade of the twenty-first century, the region experienced the ENSO phenomenon 76 percent of the time with increased severity and frequency of floods and drought (ACF-IN 2009). The increasing occurrences and severity of floods and drought do not affect everyone equally. In the soybean expansion zone and especially in the municipalities of Cuatro Cañadas and San Julián, the vast majority of small-scale farmers occupy plots of land in the flood zone around the Rio Grande, while large-scale plots occupy the more fertile and slightly higher land to the east of Highway 9.

Though deforestation due to the expansion of the agricultural frontier has been identified as a major contributor to the increasing frequency and intensity of flooding and erosion in Santa Cruz's Land Use Plan (*Plan de Uso del Suelo*), new laws have been established that excuse illegal deforestation (Law 739), increase deforestation limits (Law 741) and extend the regulatory inspections to make sure land is meeting a socioeconomic function (*Función Económica y Social*) from every two to every five years (Colque, Tinta and Sanjinés 2016). Rather than implementing strict regulations against deforestation and promoting reforestation and sustainability practices, the government is investing close to US$17 million in construction projects to protect communities and productive lands in order to facilitate the continued expansion of the agricultural frontier to serve the interests of the soy complex (ANAPO 2015). Part of these funds, however, is to be raised by the municipality with the help of medium- and large-scale farmers who remain reluctant to help the broader community if their plots are not directly threatened.

These residual solutions do not address the systemic ecological crises unfolding due to large-scale agro-industrial production and deforestation. Farmers are left with more uncertainties than ever — in terms of volatile yields due to decreasing soil fertility and increased agro-chemical requirements, drought and floods due to the ENSO system, dust storms, loss of biodiversity and an inability to diversify production and the contamination of water sources partly due to widespread fumigation.

Furthermore, a study by Mekonnen and Hoekstra (2011) of the Twente Water Centre in the Netherlands found that every ton of harvested soybeans requires a ton of water. Taking into account the total amount of forest cover lost, the decline in soil fertility, loss of biodiversity and water contamination, the result will be a stark ecological deficit and potential for ecological crisis if this production model persists. The sheer amount of agro-chemicals used in the country — 12.6 million kilograms in 2010 rising to 38.3 million kilograms in 2014 — is exhausting the soil and threatening the health and safety of communities (SENASAG 2014). The ecological extraction taking place as a result of an expanding agro-industrial soy complex is apparent.

The capitalist penetration of agriculture and the appropriation of seeds, fertilizers, pest control and even labour by industry has led to the "discontinuous but persistent undermining of discrete elements of the agricultural production process, their transformation into industrial activities, and their re-incorporation into agriculture as inputs" (Goodman, Sorj and Wilkinson

1987: 2). This process, what Goodman, Sorj and Wilkinson (1987) call appropriationism, has provoked this irreparable rift in the socioecological metabolism. The substitution of natural for industrial inputs allows for the accelerated extraction of nature's value, overriding previous ecological constraints, while the technological packages of synthetic fertilizers, GM seeds, agro-chemicals and mechanization similarly override traditional farmer knowledge, practice and labour requirements, rendering farmers increasingly dependent on or even obsolete to agro-industry. This separation and disregard for the socioecological metabolism leads to neglect of natural processes of regeneration and the symbiosis of agro-ecological processes as well as rapid environmental degradation through externalizing costs and technological fixes. Such biophysical override is unsustainable and its tendency to generate ecological crises and move into new greenfield sites exposes the accelerating contradictions of industrial capitalist agriculture (Weis 2010).

With nearly 90 percent of Bolivia's soybeans and derivatives destined for export, the ecological value is not only extracted and appropriated for value realization elsewhere; the mode of extraction diminishes the productive capacity of the natural resources in the long term, leading to ecological impoverishment and unequal ecological exchange between trading countries (Bunker 1984; see Gudynas 2015). As Bunker (1984: 1053) asserts in his important work on extractive export economies in the Amazon basin and their tendency for unequal net flows of matter and energy exchanges with productive or articulated industrial economies, "We must consider the effects of the exploitation of labor and the exploitation of the entire ecosystems as separate but complementary phenomena, both of which affect the development of particular regions." The extraction of the ecological value from the natural environment is a defining feature of agrarian extractivism in Bolivia. Over thirty years ago Bunker (1984: 1056) wrote over, "The ecological and demographic consequences of these disruptions are likely to last far longer than the demand for the commodity or the particular mode of extraction which provides it." For Bolivia, the socioeconomic and ecological impoverishment of its principal mode of extraction, mining, should serve as a stark reminder. The tragic underdevelopment and impoverishment of Bolivia's once largest and richest mining city of Potosí or the more recent disappearance of Bolivia's second-largest lake, Lago Poopó, for which hundreds of families depend for their livelihood, exemplify the harsh realities of extractivism.

Deterioration of Labour Opportunities and Conditions

The fourth dimension of agrarian extractivism in Bolivia concerns the lack of labour opportunities and deteriorating labour conditions pertaining to the soy complex. This feature refers to the issues discussed in Chapter 3 regarding productive exclusion, gender and generational forms of exclusion, toxicity and health hazards and the simple reproduction squeeze and surplus populations. This section therefore does not repeat what was covered in that chapter, but rather points to the broader trends of labour dynamics associated with agrarian extractivism.

From a labour perspective, there is nothing inherently undesirable about mechanized soybean production. To be sure, most people would much rather benefit from the increased labour productivity and less physically demanding conditions of labour associated with mechanized agriculture. In other words, it is not mechanization as a form of agricultural production that is in and of itself a problem but the social relations of production associated with the form within the broader socioeconomic context. When the form of production substantially decreases the need for labour in a sectorally and socially disarticulated economy, it can result in surplus populations (Li 2009). This dimension of agrarian extractivism is not limited to the decreased need for wage labourers in the production process, as it also relates to deteriorating conditions for workers — in terms of health, safety and precariousness. Manual sugarcane cutting in Brazil, for example, still provides a livelihood for some 500,000 people, but conditions are extremely demanding both mentally and physically, often akin to slave-like conditions (Alves 2006; McGrath 2013). Data from Brazil's Land Pastoral Commission (Comissão Pastoral da Terra) revealed that 10,010 workers were liberated from slave-like labour conditions in the sugarcane sector from 2003 to 2010 (Brasil 2011). Furthermore, in reference to oil palm and sugarcane plantations in Guatemala, Alonso-Fradejas (2015: 492) asserts that "while labor and labor arrangements are flexibly organized to maximize surplus extraction, the working conditions are damaging workers' physical and mental health in severe and even deadly ways." Both of these dimensions of labour are considered part of agrarian extractivism. In Bolivia's highly mechanized soy complex, it is labour's lack of utility for capital accumulation that is generating surplus populations.

Agrarian Extractivism and the Politics of Control

The four interlinked dimensions of agrarian extractivism expose the very extractive character of Bolivia's soy complex. Delving deeper into these extractive dynamics reveals the dimensions of power and mechanisms of access and exclusion that help us understand how the development and expansion of the agro-industrial soy complex is transforming agrarian social relations and the politics behind these processes. Building on the work of Lukes (2005) and others, the notion of power can be conceptualized with three dimensions: (1) the power to get a person or group to do something that they would not otherwise do (e.g., force), (2) the power to exclude others (e.g., regulation, market relations) and 3) the power of manipulation (e.g., legitimation, cultural hegemony) (Lukes 2005; Gaventa 1980; Hall, Hirsch and Li 2011). These dimensions of power are distinct yet interrelated. For example, people may be forcibly displaced from their lands by a politically connected agro-industrial corporation or capitalist elite that is able to negotiate with state authorities for a legal land concession over the area, which, as far as the courts are concerned, legitimizes their formal right to the land and manipulates perceptions regarding the initial expulsion. This hypothetical situation demonstrates how these three dimensions overlap and can reinforce one another as "bundles of power" (Ribot and Peluso 2003: 154). Ribot and Peluso's (2003) structural and relational mechanisms of access encompass a range of powers that affect people's ability to benefit from resources. These include technology, capital, markets, labour and labour opportunities, knowledge, authority, social identities and social relations, which can shape patterns of benefit distribution. Most of these structural and relational mechanisms of access are within the first and second dimensions of power. Access to knowledge, as explained by Ribot and Peluso (2003: 168), includes "beliefs, ideological controls and discursive practices, as well as negotiated systems of meanings" and is therefore understood within the third dimension of power.

The mechanisms of access associated with Bolivia's soy complex are mostly within the second dimension of power (see Table 5.1). However, as Colque (2014) points out, agro-capitalist elites do appropriate land illegally via their position of authority on the frontier, where state authority is largely absent and landed elites are able to use force to extend their landholdings. Further, particularly in the mid-2000s when soybean plantations were expanding rapidly, many smallholders were forced to substitute soybean monocultures for traditional crop production, whether they wanted to or not. Many were attracted to the idea of modernizing their smallholding

Table 5.1 Power, Exclusion and Access Mechanisms

	First dimension of power	Second dimension of power	Third dimension of power
Characteristics	Force, negotiation	Market forces, institutional barriers, exclusion	Manipulation, legitimacy, cultural hegemony, war of position
Powers of exclusion	Force	Markets, regulation	Legitimation
Access mechanisms	Authority	Technology, capital, markets, labour, authority, identity, social relations	Knowledge

Source: Author's elaboration based on Lukes 2005; Hall, Hirsch and Li 2011; Ribot and Peluso 2003.

complete with mechanized production and high-yielding seed varieties (GM) and their necessary technological packages. Others, like Mrs. Choque, mentioned in Chapter 3, were forced to switch to GM soybean cultivation due to widespread contamination of their lands, whether by airplane fumigation or agro-chemical run-off in their soil and water sources. In other words, people can be forced to do something that they would not otherwise do by means other than physical displacement or violence.

Another example, which demonstrates the first dimension of power, is access to those with authority. Personnel from the Natural Disasters and Risk Management Unit (Gestion de Riesgos y Desastres Naturales) for the Municipality of San Julián receive regular complaints regarding the construction of illegal dams and river diversions, which flood neighbouring parcels, in violation of Law 2140, Article 17, which prohibits such action. The majority of these complaints are made by smallholders against agribusiness companies. However, many of these companies are economically and politically influential, with connections at the regional or even national governmental level. State actors, such as those at the Natural Disaster Unit in San Julián, have very limited capacity to act against such large and influential companies. As one member of the Natural Disaster Unit put it in conversation with me:

> Even us at the municipal government level cannot change this. They [agribusinesses] are too powerful for us. We try to make

> them pay fines, to comply by the law, but they don't listen. And what can we do? They have connections with higher authorities that override us.

In this case, it is access to authority (first dimension of power) that gives agribusinesses the power to divert rivers or build dams illegally without repercussions that apply to the rest of society. Most access mechanisms and powers of exclusion associated with the soy complex fall within the second dimension of power. The capital-intensive form of soybean production requires access to technologies, capital and markets, thus excluding the rural majority. It further excludes and outright eliminates access to labour opportunities. Yet smallholders are encouraged to integrate and engage in value-chain relations as recommended by the World Bank with its residual approach to poverty reduction. This perspective condemns the use of illegitimate force (first dimension), enables the power of the market to allocate people, goods and services efficiently and effectively (second dimension) and fails to question the underlying logics of this type of development (third dimension). Without questioning the market logic, these approaches assume that integrating people within existing market relations will lead to development and poverty reduction. But how did this logic of development become part of the state's dominant discourse and gain legitimacy in Bolivia — a country with the concepts of *vivir bien*, rights to Mother Nature and food sovereignty written in its Constitution?

Rather than challenge the mechanisms of exclusion that marginalize the rural majority and the MAS party's main constituents (Indigenous-peasants), elected state actors representing MAS formed a state-capital alliance in Santa Cruz in order to maintain their political power and control over the state apparatus, while allowing landed elites and agro-capitalists to maintain and gain more control over land-based resources in the lowlands. As Bolivia's former vice minister of land, Alejandro Almaraz (2014: 54), put it, "The indigenous and peasant project ... has been defeated, and the dominant interests and power of the business sector, the oligarchs and the latifundistas have been reinstalled." Legal reforms such as the extension of the *Función Económica y Social*, a lenient deforestation code and pardons for illegal deforestation, a non-retroactive land ceiling law, the abandonment of agrarian reform, more stringent penalties against land occupations, the legalization of extraction within formerly protected Indigenous territories, the push to legalize all transgenic crops at the 2015 Agricultural Summit, the US$700 million annual diesel subsidy that largely benefits agro-industry rather than the rural majority and the commitment to expand the agricultural frontier for agro-industrial development are evidence of this new state–agro-capital alliance that has emerged (Almaraz 2015).

Walter Chavez (2013), a former advisor to Morales and now critic of MAS, describes this process as struggle-victory-inclusion-expansion. "Struggle" is in reference to the struggle for state power pre- and post-2006, while victory refers to the overwhelming support of MAS in the 2006 national elections and the 2008 referendum. "Inclusion and expansion" refers to the necessity of including the influential Santa Cruz elites within the MAS political agenda in order to expand the government's political reach and maintain state power. State discourses and meetings between the MAS political executive and the Santa Cruz elite have made it increasingly clear that a new relationship has developed between the state and agro-capital (Webber 2016; see Viaña 2012). These changes in the state-society-capital nexus should not be understood as the state actions and autonomous decision-making of a unified bureaucratic machine, but rather outcomes that reflect the balance of forces in society and class struggle. As explained in Chapter 3, the particular class positions of the masses characterized as functional dualism enabled the state to form this alliance without entering into a crisis of legitimacy.

These class and political dynamics of agrarian change have enabled agro-industry to increase its control over Bolivia's land-based natural resources. Agro-industrial companies not only have a market oligopoly over upstream and downstream components but also largely control research and development and therefore access to knowledge. This allows them to set research and development agendas to serve their accumulation interests, and effectively control the mechanisms within the third dimension of power. The result is agrarian extractivism.

Agrarian extractivism extracts raw materials in high volumes destined for export, controlled by a market oligopoly that appropriates the surplus value from labour and nature without creating value-added sectoral linkages with the domestic economy. It further removes labour opportunities and contributes to environmental degradation. The structural and relational mechanisms of access, which span the three dimensions of power, thus enable agro-industry to appropriate surplus value and retain the benefits from soybean production without necessarily owning the land. Discourses from the state and oilseed producer associations continue to promote the expansion of the agricultural frontier for food sovereignty, food security, rural employment and development (Vicepresidente 2012; IBCE 2014). Elected state actors and classes of capital in Santa Cruz used these legitimating discourses to maintain their control over the state apparatus and the soy complex, respectively. The lack of resistance, due to a variety of historical and cultural factors previously discussed but also the constraints of functional dualism, has enabled classes of capital to gain and maintain control over land-based natural resources and the soy complex at the expense of the rural majority and the natural environment. For MAS, it was not worth the political and economic risks of challenging the land-based wealth and power of classes of capital in Santa Cruz since social forces were not mobilized from below. Furthermore, without resistance and social organization, the state does not have the capacity to undertake pro-poor agrarian reform or challenge the logic of the agro-industrial soy complex, but rather requires the mutually reinforcing synergies from pro-reformist actors from below (Fox 1993; Borras 2007).

While state actors certainly have some autonomy and capacity through their individual agencies, the state as an ensemble of contested social relations does not exercise power just as it pleases, but works through the balance of class forces in society. With the balance of forces in Santa Cruz heavily in favour of agro-capitalist and landed elites with very little resistance, the MAS government had very little to gain and much to lose if transformative policy changes were pursued. As Fox (1993: 22) puts it, "State action is the result of a reciprocal cause and effect relationship between changes in the balance of power within the state and shifts in the balance of power within society." This is why resistance from below is so important if the extractive character of the soy complex is to be dismantled and transformed. Yet the legitimacy of the agro-industrial model of development is deeply entrenched within the power structures and access mechanisms, not only in Bolivia but at the global level with increasingly concentrated control over the global food system. Without challenging the logic and underlying power relations of the agro-industrial soy complex, processes of exclusion, value appropriation and environmental degradation are likely to continue leading to a truncated trajectory of agrarian change.

Conclusion

The new extractivism cannot solely be characterized by the increased role of the state in appropriating rents from key sectors of the extractive economy to redistribute to the masses in the form of social welfare programs. Indeed, the new extractivism in Latin America generally suggests an increased role for the state, but that increased role can also appear in different forms in order to increase not only economic control but also political control over the territory. The decisions not to pursue redistributive agrarian reform, to strengthen private property, to loosen the deforestation code and to facilitate agro-industry's expansion of the agricultural frontier were the result of the relational dynamics of the state-society-capital nexus. To avoid potential class warfare and a loss of state power, elected state managers representing MAS opted for a class alliance with classes of capital represented by the Santa Cruz landed and industrial elites. This decision was a response to the economic strength of the Media Luna's capitalist classes, which, in years prior, had threatened to separate from the country in a violent coup.

In this chapter, I have exposed the socioeconomic and environmental implications of the development and expansion of the soy complex, revealing its extractive character and the politics behind these processes. I have argued that rather than a form of agro-industrialization, the soy complex in Bolivia is better characterized as agrarian extractivism. As a concept, agrarian extractivism is both politically and analytically useful for understanding new dynamics of agrarian change brought on by this type of capitalist agricultural development. It directly challenges the notion of agro-industrialization by exposing the lack of industrial linkages, employment generation and benefits for the domestic economy. Agrarian extractivism should be understood within the context of the broader neo-extractivist development model. As a self-proclaimed government of social movements, MAS maintained its legitimacy and control over the state apparatus by using extractivist rents to fund social welfare programs. Though the soy complex does not generate significant revenues for the state, it allows for a similar balance of capital accumulation and political legitimacy as that generated by the other extractive sectors.

The balance of forces in society has not undergone the same shift as that which took place in the mining and hydrocarbon sectors. The history of organized mobilization among miners established their position as a powerful societal force. This shift forced the state to grant concessions to mining cooperatives and the state mining company or risk a crisis of legitimacy. The politics of natural gas were at the heart of the Gas War, which, among other factors, led to the election of Morales and MAS with their discourses of resource nationalism (Pellegrini 2016; see Arsel et al. 2014). In other words, these other pillars of the state's three-pronged extractivist development strategy have been highly politicized, with societal forces struggling to change the balance of powers underlying the relations of access and control over these resources. In the lowlands of Santa Cruz, such dynamics did not take shape. Despite the unequal agrarian structure, smallholders became integrated into the soy complex, then excluded and caught in relations of debt and dependency. The soy complex achieved a high degree of legitimacy even among those it excluded and marginalized. As such, the balance of capital accumulation and legitimacy is once again maintained, but under different circumstances. Legitimacy is maintained through discourses of modernization, food security, food sovereignty and rural development and through the contradictory class positions of smallholders engaged in the soy complex, while accumulation interests of classes of capital are maintained without state interference.

Discrepancies and contradictions between the trajectory of agrarian change of the agro-industrial development model and the government's overall stated rural development model objectives are becoming more apparent. The objectives of MAS's productive revolution and the New Economic, Social, Communitarian and Productive Model were to develop the agricultural sector as an income- and employment-generating strategic sector (Arce Catacora 2011). As this book has revealed, the extractive features of agro-industrial development exclude the rural majority and threaten future farming prospects through environmental degradation, while surplus value (primarily in the form of ground rent) is appropriated by an agro-industrial market oligopoly. Yet the social inclusiveness (cash transfers) of the neo-extractivist development model, combined with smallholder rentierism through the *partida* arrangement, has enabled the persistence of smallholders in the soy complex despite being stripped of access mechanisms and excluded from the production process. Underlying such an apparently inclusive rural development model are hidden forms of exclusion, which are slowly leading to the disappearance of smallholders and a further concentration of power and resource control within the agrarian sector. The extractivist dynamics of agro-industrial development are therefore eroding and contradicting the stated objectives of the MAS government's broader national development strategy. Such residual approaches to poverty reduction have been quite successful in the short term and in the context of extremely favourable international commodity prices, but structural inequalities persist and such contradictions are beginning to surface as commodity prices have fallen, environmental crises become more frequent and productive exclusion leads to dispossession. These dynamics reflect the broader contradictions inherent in the state's neo-extractivist model and help explain, in part, the widespread discontent among the masses and the recent legitimacy crisis faced by the Morales government, which ultimately led to its downfall. These are the dynamics of the politics of control associated with Bolivia's soy complex.

NOTES

1. Converted to US dollars at a rate of 1 USD = 6.89 Bs. Original data from source is Bs 40.543 billion in 2005 to Bs 221.181 billion in 2015 (MEFP 2015).
2. Alonso-Fradejas (2015) puts forth a working definition of a financialized and flexible type of agrarian extractivism in Guatemala characterized by a knowledge and metabolic rift, limited wage work opportunities and poor working conditions and the appropriation of the surplus value and land rent by financialized capitals.
3. For conceptualizations and uses of the concept across various contexts and crop complexes, see McKay, Alonso-Fradejas and Ezquerro-Cañete (2020).
4. Data based on summer harvest only.

REFERENCES

ACF-IN. 2009. *Santa Cruz: Plan departamental de contingencias para desastres naturales*. Santa Cruz.

Acosta, Alberto. 2013. "Extractivism and Neo Extractivism: Two Sides of the Same Curse." In Mariam Lang and Dunia Mokrani (eds.), *Beyond Development: Alternative Visions from Latin America*. Amsterdam: Transnational Institute.

Almaraz, Alejandro. 2014. "Las Luchas Indígenas y Campesinas En Los Dos Ciclos de La Reforma Agraria." In Fundación TIERRA (ed.), *Recientes Transformaciones Agrarias En Bolivia: Memoria*. La Paz: Fundación TIERRA.

____. 2015. "El MAS Abraza El Model Capitalista." *Petropress*.

Alonso-Fradejas, Alberto. 2015. "Anything but a Story Foretold: Multiple Politics of Resistance to the Agrarian Extractivist Project in Guatemala." *Journal of Peasant Studies*, 42, 3–4: 489–515.

Alves, Francisco. 2006. "Por Que Morrem Os Cortadores de Cana?" *Saude e Sociedade*, 15, 3: 90–98.

ANAPO. 2015. *Memoria Anual 2015*. Santa Cruz: Asociacion de Productores de Oleaginosas y Trigo.

Arce Catacora, Luis Alberto. 2011. *El Nuevo Modelo Económico, Social, Comunitario y Productivo*. La Paz.

Arsel, Murat. 2012. "Between 'Marx and Markets'? The State, the 'Left Turn' and Nature in Ecuador." *Tijdschrift Voor Economische En Sociale Geografie*, 103, 2: 150–163.

Arsel, Murat, Barbara Hogenboom, and Lorenzo Pellegrini. 2016. "The Political Economy of the Extractive Imperative in Latin America." *The Extractive Industries and Society*, 3: 880–887. Elsevier Ltd.

Arsel, Murat, Carlos Mena, Lorenzo Pellegrini, and Isabella Radhuber. 2014. "Property Rights, Nationalisation and Extractive Industries in Bolivia and Ecuador." In Maarten Bavinck, Lorenzo Pellegrini, and Erik Mostert (eds.), *Conflict on Natural Resources in the Global South — Conceptual Approaches*. Leiden: CRC Press/Balkema.

Bebbington, Anthony J. 2009. "The New Extraction: Rewriting the Political Ecology of the Andes?" NACLA *Report on the Americas*, 42, 5: 12–20.

Bebbington, Anthony, and Denise Humphreys Bebbington. 2011. "An Andean Avatar: Post-Neoliberal and Neoliberal Strategies for Securing the Unobtainable."

New Political Economy, 16 (May): 131–145.
Bernstein, Henry. 2010. *Class Dynamics of Agrarian Change*. Halifax and Winnipeg: Fernwood Publishing.
BID. 2014. *Perfil de Risego de Desastres Para Bolivia Ante Inundaciones y Deslizamientos En Cuencas Seleccionadas*. Washington, DC.
Borras, Saturnino M. Jr. 2007. *Pro-Poor Land Reform: A Critique*. Ottawa: University of Ottawa Press.
Bradshaw, C.J.A., N.S. Sodhi, K.S.H. Peh, and B.W. Brook. 2007. "Global Evidence That Deforestation Amplifies Flood Risk and Severity in the Developing World." *Global Change Biology*, 13, 11: 2379–2395.
Brasil, Reporter. 2011. "Brazil's Ethanol in the World: Socio-Environmental Impacts of Export Sugarcane Companies." *Evaluation*, 20.
Bunker, Stephen G. 1984. "Modes of Extraction, Unequal Exchange, and the Progressive Underdevelopment of an Extreme Periphery: The Brazilian Amazon, 1600–1980." *American Journal of Sociology*, 89, 5: 1017.
Campanini, Jorge. 2015. *El Decreto 2366 Dicta La Sentencia a Las Áreas Protegidas En Bolivia*. Cochabamba.
Catacora-Vargas, Georgina, Pablo Galeano, Sarah Zanon Agapito-Tenfen, Darìo Aranda, Tomàs Palau, and Rubens Onofre Nodari. 2012. *Soybean Production in the Southern Cone of the Americas: Update on Land and Pesticide Use*. Norway: GenOk — Centre for Biosafety.
Chase-Dunn, C., and T.D. Hall. 2000. "Comparing World-Systems to Explain Social Evolution." In R.A. Denemark, J. Friedman, B.K. Gills, and G. Modelski (eds.), *World System History: The Social Science of Long-Term Change*. London and New York: Routledge.
Chavez, Walter. 2013. "Evo, Santa Cruz y La Revolución." *El Desacuerdo*.
Colque, Gonzalo. 2014. *Expanión de la Frontera Agrícola: Luchas por el Control y Apropiación de la Tierra en el Oriente Boliviano*. La Paz: TIERRA.
Colque, Gonzalo, Efraín Tinta, and Esteban Sanjinés. 2016. *Segunda Reforma Agraria: Una Historia que Incomoda*. La Paz: TIERRA.
Corz, Carlos. 2016. "García Linera Dice Que Bolivia Ganó Una Década y Perfila 20 Años de Extractivismo." *La Razón Digital*, August 18.
Cuéllar, S., A. Rodríguez, J. Arroyo, S. Espinoza, and D. Larrea. 2012. *Mapa de Deforestación de Las Tierras Bajas y Los Yungas de Bolivia 2000–2005–2010: Proyección Sistema de Coordenadas Geográficas, Datum WGS84*. Santa Cruz de la Sierra.
de Janvry, Alain. 1981. *The Agrarian Question and Reformism in Latin America*. Baltimore: Johns Hopkins University Press.
ECLAC (Economic Commission for Latin America and the Caribbean). 2014. *Statistical Yearbook for Latin America and the Caribbean*. Santiago.
EM-DAT. 2016. "Emergency Events Database."
Fearnside, Philip M. 1989. "Extractive Reservices in Brazilian Amazonia." *BioScience*, 39, 6: 387–393.
____. 2001. "Soybean Cultivation as a Threat to the Environment in Brazil." *Environmental Conservation*, 28, 01: 23–38.
Fine, Ben, and Alfredo Saad Filho. 2004. *Marx's Capital*, 4th ed. Lond and Sterling.

Virginia: Pluto Press.
Fox, Jonathan. 1993. *The Politics of Food in Mexico*. Ithaca and London: Cornell University Press.
Fuentes, Federico. 2011. "Bolivia: Against 'Green Imperialism.'" *Monthly Review*. <mronline.org/2011/09/25/bolivia-against-green-imperialism>
Fundación Jubileo. 2016. *Reporte de Las Industrias Extractivas En Bolivia*. La Paz.
García Linera, Álvaro. 2012. *Geopolitics of the Amazon*, edited by Richard Fidler. Climateandcapitalism.com.
____. 2013. "Once Again on So-Called 'Extractivism.'" *Monthly Review*.
Gaventa, John. 1980. "Power and Powerlessness: Quiescence and Rebellion in an Appalachian Valley." *Perspective*, 288.
Giarracca, N., and M. Teubal. 2014. "Argentina: Extractivist Dynamics of Soy Production and Open-Pit Mining." In Henry Veltmeyer and James Petras (eds.), *The New Extractivism: A Post-Neoliberal Development Model or Imperialism of the Twenty-First Century?* London: Zed Books.
Goodman, David, Bernardo Sorj, and John Wilkinson. 1987. *From Farming to Biotechnology: A Theory of Agro-Industrial Development*. Oxford, UK: Basil Blackwell.
Gudynas, Eduardo. 2009. "Diez Tesis Urgentes Sobre El Nuevo Extractivismo. Contextos y Demandas Bajo El Progresismo Sudamericano Actual." In *Extractivismo, Política y Sociedad*. Quito: Centro Andino de Acción Popular y Centro Latino Americano de Ecología Social.
____. 2010a. "The New Extractivism of the 21st Century: Ten Urgent Theses about Extractivism in Relation to Current South American Progressivism." *Americas Program Report*, January 21: 1–14.
____. 2010b. "Agropecuaria y Nuevo Extractivismo Bajo Los Gobiernos Progresistas de América Del Sur." *Territorios*, 5: 37–54.
____. 2013. "Extracciones, Extractivismos y Extrahecciones." *Observatorio Del Desarrollo*, 18: 1–18.
____. 2015. *Extractivismos: Ecología, Economía y Política de Un Modo de Entender El Desarollo y La Naturaleza*. Cochabamba: CEDIB.
Hall, Derek, Philip Hirsch, and Tania Murray Li. 2011. *Powers of Exclusion: Land Dilemmas in Southeast Asia*. Singapore and Honolulu: NUS Press and University of Hawaii Press.
Harvey, David. 2006. *The Limits Capital*. London: Verso.
Hecht, Susanna B. 2005. "Soybeans, Development and Conservation on the Amazon Frontier." *Development and Change*, 36, 2: 375–404.
Heredia Garcia, H. 2014. "Gobierno se Abre a Construir La Agenda Del Millon de Ha." *El Deber*. Santa Cruz de la Sierra.
IBCE. 2014. *Soya : Su Importancia Como Cadena de Valor Agroproductiva En Bolivia*, 227. Santa Cruz: Instituto Boliviano de Comercio Exterior.
____. 2015. *Cifras Del Comercio Exterior Boliviano*, 229. Santa Cruz.
Kay, Cristóbal. 1989. *Latin American Theories of Development and Underdevelopment*. London: Routledge.
Lazcano, M. 2013. "Estado Boliviano Controla El 38% de La Economia." *La Razón*.
Li, Tania Murray. 2009. "To Make Live or Let Die? Rural Dispossession and the

Protection of Surplus Populations." *Antipode*, 41, S1: 66–93.
Lukes, Steven. 2005. *Power: A Radical View*, second ed. New York: Palgrave Macmillan.
Malhi, Y., J. Timmons Roberts, R.A. Betts, T.J. Killeen, W. Li, and C.A. Nobre. 2008. "Climate Change, Deforestation, and the Fate of the Amazon." *Science*, 319, 5860: 169–172.
Marx, Karl. 1976. *Capital: A Critque of Political Economy, Volume One*. Middlesex, England: Penguin Books.
____. 1981. *Capital: A Critique of Political Economy, Volume Three*. London: Penguin Books.
McGrath, S. 2013. "Fuelling Global Production Networks with Slave Labour?: Migrant Sugar Cane Workers in the Brazilian Ethanol GPN." *Geoforum*, 44: 32–43.
McKay, Ben M., Alberto Alonso-Fradejas, and Arturo Ezquerro-Cañete. 2020. *Agrarian Extractivism in Latin America*. London and New York: Routledge.
MEFP. 2015. *Proyecto Presupuesto General Del Estado Gestion 2016*. La Paz.
Mekonnen, M.M., and A.Y. Hoekstra. 2011. "The Green, Blue and Grey Water Footprint of Crops and Derived Crop Products." *Hydrology and Earth System Sciences*, 15, 5: 1577–1600.
Müller, Robert, Daniel M. Larrea-Alcázar, Saul Cuéllar, and Sara Espinoza. 2014. "Causas Directas de La Deforestación Reciente (2000–2010) y Modelado de Dos Escenarios Futuros En Las Tierras Bajas de Bolivia Lowlands and Modeling of Future Scenarios." *Ecología En Bolivia*, 49, 1: 20–34.
Müller, Robert, Till Pistorius, Sophia Rohde, Gerhard Gerold, and Pablo Pacheco. 2013. "Policy Options to Reduce Deforestation Based on a Systematic Analysis of Drivers and Agents in Lowland Bolivia." *Land Use Policy*, 30, 1: 895–907.
Pellegrini, Lorenzo. 2016. "Resource Nationalism in the Plurinational State of Bolivia." In Paul A. Haslam and Pablo Heidrich (eds.), *The Political Economy of Resources and Development: From Neoliberalism to Resource Nationalism*. London: Routledge.
Pengue, W.A. 2005. "Transgenic Crops in Argentina: The Ecological and Social Debt." *Bulletin of Science, Technology & Society*, 25, 4: 314–322.
Petras, James, and Henry Veltmeyer. 2014. *Extractive Imperialism in the Americas: Capitalism's New Frontier*. Leiden and Boston: Brill.
____. 2016. *Power and Resistance: US Imperialism in Latin America*. Leiden: Koninklijke Brill.
Ribot, Jesse C., and Nancy Lee Peluso. 2003. "A Theory of Access." *Rural Sociology*, 68, 2: 153–181.
Schmidt-Bleek, Friedrich. 1999. *The Factor 10/MIPS-Concept: Bridging Ecological, Economic, and Social Dimensions with Sustainability Indicators*. Tokyo.
SENASAG. 2014. "Database: Servicio Nacional de Sanidad Agropecuaria e Inocuidad Alimentaria."
Seoane, J., E. Taddei, and C. Algranati. 2013. *Extractivismo, Despojo y Crisis Climatica: Desafios Para Lost Movimientos Sociales y Los Proyectos Emancipatorios de Nuestra America*. Buenos Aires: Ediciones Herramiento.
Svampa, Maristella. 2013. "Resource Extractivism and Alternatives: Latin American Perspectives on Development." In M. Lang and D. Mokrani (eds.), *Beyond*

Development: Alternative Visions from Latin America. Amsterdam and Quito: Transnational Institute and Rosa Luxemburg Foundation.
Vadillo, Alcides, Jorge M. Salgado, and Simar N. Muiba. 2013. *Gobernanza de Los Recursos Naturales En Lomerío*. La Paz: Fundaction TIERRA.
Varela Mendoza, E. 2014. "El Estado Controla 43 Empresas En Bolivia." *El Deber*.
Veltmeyer, Henry. 2013. "The Political Economy of Natural Resource Extraction: A New Model or Extractive Imperialism?" *Canadian Journal of Development Studies-Revue Canadienne D Etudes Du Developpement*, 34, 1: 79–95.
____. 2016. "Extractive Capital, the State and the Resistance in Latin America." *Sociology and Anthropology*, 4, 8: 774–784.
Veltmeyer, Henry, and James Petras. 2014. *The New Extractivism: A Post-Neoliberal Development Model or Imperialism of the Twenty-First Century?* London: Zed Books.
Viaña, Jorge. 2012. "Estado Plurinacional y Nueva Fase Del Proceso Boliviano." In Mabel Thwaites Rey (ed.), *El Estado En América Latina: Continuidades y Rupturas*. Santiago del Chile: CLACSO.
Vicepresidente. 2012. "Gobierno y CAO Acuerdan Ampliar La Frontera Agricola Para Garantizar Soberanía Alimentaria." *Vicepresidencia Del Estado Plurinacional de Bolivia*.
Villegas, Pablo. 2015. "Lo Que Tiene Que Pasar, Pasa! La Crisis de Las Materias Primas." *Petropress*, 35: 41–55.
Webber, Jeffery R. 2016. "Evo Morales and the Political Economy of Passive Revolution in Bolivia, 2006–15." *Third World Quarterly*, 37, 10: 1855–1876.
Weis, Tony. 2010. "The Accelerating Biophysical Contradictions of Industrial Capitalist Agriculture." *Journal of Agrarian Change*, 10, 3: 315–341.
____. 2013. "The Meat of the Global Food Crisis." *Journal of Peasant Studies*, 40, 1: 65–85.

Conclusion

Bolivia's soy complex is leading to new forms and mechanisms of exclusion, value-chain control, surplus appropriation and extraction, which further marginalize and subordinate the rural majority. Processes of productive exclusion have divorced smallholders from their land, not to the extent of displacing them but impeding access to the necessary means to put their land into production. Those who are not excluded and are working their land are caught in value-chain relations of debt and dependency. At both ends of the value chain, a market oligopoly controls the upstream and downstream components of the soy complex, appropriating the majority of the surplus value produced. Contrary to claims contending that this type of agricultural development model is beneficial for the economy, employment generation, food security and even food sovereignty, this study has revealed its exclusive and extractivist character — socially, economically and environmentally. The politics of control, as an analytical framework, has helped us understand the contested nature of the state and the relations between state, societal and capitalist actors, revealing the emergence of a state-capital alliance enabled by particular class relations and contradictions in society. The remainder of this chapter elaborates on the main conclusions and points to some implications of this study for researchers, policymakers and social movements.

New Dynamics of Control, Exclusion and Extraction

If one were to apply the Food and Agriculture Organization of the United Nations' original formulation of land grabs to analyze the dynamics of agrarian change in Bolivia, the conclusion would be that land-grabbing is not taking place and food security is not threatened (Soto Baquero and Gómez 2012: 560). Furthermore, if one were to read the reports published by ANAPO and the Bolivian Institute of Foreign Trade and listen to the discourses of the MAS executive such as former vice president García Linera, one might conclude that the soy complex is creating tens of thousands of jobs, providing a livelihood for thousands of small farmers who make up the majority of soybean producers (78 percent), contributing to the country's food security and even food sovereignty. The World Bank would certainly applaud these initiatives, pointing to their conclusions in the *World Development Report 2008*, where they recommended the integration of smallholders into agro-industrial value-chain relations.

This book, however, challenges these claims and exposes how these dominant discourses and narratives are misleading and can often lead to exclusion and marginalization. A property rights approach does not capture the processes of productive exclusion nor the forms of value chain control discussed in Chapter 4. The more nuanced characterization of contemporary land grabs as control grabbing put forth by Borras et al. (2012) and Ribot and Peluso's (2003) theory of access capture these changes in the social relations of production, property and power in the contemporary period. The lack of certain structural and relational access mechanisms prevents smallholders from benefitting from the fruits of their land, not only representing powers of exclusion but also forms of control and adverse incorporation, hindering class consciousness and organized forms of social mobilization. The lack of access to capital, technology and credit deprive capital-poor smallholders from putting their land into production, thereby forcing them to rent their land and find alternative means of income generation. But the mechanisms of exclusion and control run deeper than having access to capital or credit. Those farmers able to put land into production enter into value-chain relations of debt and dependency within a corporate-controlled market oligopoly. These farmers bear all the risk and their income is increasingly jeopardized by volatile and uncertain yields, natural disasters, increased production costs and the presence of new pests and weeds. While they are able to retain relatively more benefits than semiproletarian and petty bourgeois rentiers, they also risk entering into debt relations where they become controlled by agro-industry's standards, credit and markets due to input-harvest debt relations. But beyond those capital-poor smallholders and those capital-rich farmers integrated into the value chain, this study has revealed the extractive character of the soy complex, which has important socioeconomic and environmental implications for society.

I argue for the need to start reframing certain types of so-called industrial agriculture as agrarian extractivism. It is important to reveal the very extractive dynamics of agricultural production and stop serving legitimating discourses often used by agribusiness and states alike that equate this type of agricultural production to industrialization. Corporate control over the food system, both upstream and downstream, capital's subsumption of labour and the increased appropriation (and extraction) of nature's value in the production process by means of agro-chemical inputs, heavy machinery and deforestation for frontier expansion should not be characterized as industrialization but as extraction. The influence and power of agribusiness over research and development, fuelled by neo-Malthusian discourses on the need to feed a growing population, has equipped the agro-industrial model with legitimacy and authority in the countryside. Agrarian extractivism forces us to go beyond oversimplified dichotomies of large versus small scale, GM versus agro-ecology, and to not group all types of industrial agriculture together. It forces us to delve more deeply into an analysis of the relations of production, distribution, consumption and accumulation and the associated environmental implications. It implies engaging with structural and relational access mechanisms by going beyond property rights and the origin of capital and revealing the broader socioeconomic and environmental implications of capital penetration and new forms of production.

The Politics of Control: Power, Access and the State

By contextualizing the development of Bolivia's agrarian structure historically, this study has shown how forms of exclusion and mechanisms of control have changed over time, from authority and force, markets and regulation, to legitimacy and consent. The underlying dimensions of power, control and access mechanisms have been analyzed in relation to the state-society-capital nexus, as the balance of forces in society help us understand political and socioeconomic change. The politics of control, as the overarching analytical framework guiding this study, has captured the new forms and mechanisms of resource control and value appropriation (or extraction) in (agro-)extractive sectors through an analysis of access rather than property or concessional rights. These include various forms of dispossession and displacement but also mechanisms of exclusion and appropriation that do not necessarily require the physical removal of people from the land or formal ownership of property rights. The politics of control also provides an analytical framework for evaluating the state's dual and often contradictory functions of facilitating capital accumulation and maintaining political legitimacy and the strategic relations between state and societal actors in gaining and maintaining control over the state apparatus. Using this framework to analyze the development and expansion of the agro-industrial soy complex in Bolivia has revealed how problematic this dominant development model can be for the rural majority, the environment and the domestic economy. Productivity gains and economic growth are not trickling down to the rural poor, instead leading to exclusion, value appropriation and extraction. The integration of smallholders into value-chain relations as recommended in the World Bank's (2007) *World Development Report 2008* dismisses the very structural and relational access mechanisms associated with production, property and power analyzed in this study. Taking a relational approach, this study challenges the agro-industrial logic of development, revealing its extractive dynamics and detrimental impacts on domestic economies, employment opportunities and the natural environment.

The dynamics of exclusion, value appropriation and extraction are not unique to the agro-industrial soy complex, but rather systemic features of agro-industry's development model. The industrial components are via appropriationism and substitutionism, not through sectoral linkages and value-added industrial production (Goodman, Sorj and Wilkinson 1987). Furthermore, as Tony Weis (2010: 316) explains, the agro-industrial model is wearing away the biophysical foundations of agriculture through "soil erosion and salinization; the overdraft of water and threats to its long-term supply; the loss of biodiversity and crucial 'ecosystem services' (e.g., pollination, soil formation); and greenhouse gas (GHG) emissions." The agro-industrial bias in the national policies of many nation-states, particularly in the Global North, and the increasing concentration of control by the Big Four agro-chemical companies upstream and the ABCD agro-industrial companies downstream has led not only to a market oligopoly conducive to price fixing and limited consumer choices but to corporate control and dominance over research and development, agricultural knowledge and authority. The threats this presents go beyond those of markets and regulations to legitimacy through manufacturing consent. It is urgent and pertinent that we continue to critically examine the socioeconomic and environmental implications of agro-industrial development around the world so as to not take for granted the legitimacy claimed by a corporate oligopoly–controlled research and development agenda for agro-industrial development. As this study has shown, it is crucial to go beyond a property rights–based approach centred on land as well as an exclusive focus on the origins of capital (i.e., foreignization) to the forms and mechanisms of exclusion, control, surplus appropriation and extraction associated with capital penetration. In order to fully grasp these new dynamics of agrarian change, we must engage not only with aspects of accumulation but also the new forms and relations of production and the role and nature of the state in their historical formations. Particularly in the current context of the resource rush, new and changing dynamics of agrarian change triggered by the capitalist development of the countryside highlight the relevance of re-engaging with contemporary agrarian questions of capital and labour (Akram-Lodhi and Kay 2009).

While it is clear that in many parts of the world, capital is taking hold of and revolutionizing agriculture through the commodification of production, it is highly uneven and variegated, taking different forms over different historical periods. In the contemporary period of industrial value-chain agriculture and global capitalism, this study has revealed some of those forms and the dynamics of agrarian change that have emerged in the context of the soy complex in Bolivia. Its capital-intensive form is exclusive, while industrial capital's concentration of control over the upstream and downstream components have not only created new spaces for capital accumulation but appropriated the majority of the surplus value without the need to have formal ownership or nominal rights over the land. Smallholders representing the rural majority have become adversely incorporated into these new value-chain relations, caught in contradictory class positions that hinder class consciousness and organized forms of resistance.

These new forms of capital penetration are shaping, and are being shaped by, the political dynamics of agrarian change characterized by the functional dualism that has emerged in the countryside. It is in the interest of capital for smallholders to remain on the land. If the majority of smallholders are eventually dispossessed due to the simple reproduction squeeze discussed in Chapter 3, surplus populations could emerge and threaten the state-capital alliance, disrupting the fine balance of accumulation and legitimacy. As an analytical framework, the politics of control captures these dynamics of production, accumulation and political formations in their context-specific and historically situated contexts. Beyond the soy complex and dynamics of agrarian change specific to Bolivia, the politics of control as an analytical framework for agrarian political economy can be used across sectors and geographic areas to analyze the socioeconomic and political dynamics of agrarian change. Whether it is sugarcane in Brazil, China or southern Africa, oil palm in Indonesia, Colombia or Nigeria, maize in the United States or Mexico, the politics of control as a framework of analysis can help us understand how new forms of capital penetration are leading agrarian transformation and the implications for society, the economy and the environment. The new ways that capital is penetrating the agricultural sector and new actors involved demand a deeper understanding of how these processes are shaping the social relations of production, property and power.

The Bolivian case presented here demonstrates new forms of covert, adverse incorporation, leading to a truncated trajectory of agrarian change. Smallholders are excluded but officially remain classified as small-scale farmers in the soybean sector. The very extractive character of new types of so-called industrial value-chain agriculture is not resulting in any type of industrialization in the home market. Rather, the industrial components are manufactured elsewhere and industrial capital seeks new spaces and sites to circulate, produce and extract surplus value. Just as the capital-intensive form of production shapes the relations of production, it also shapes political formations in the countryside. The Bolivian case demonstrates the lack of organized "class for itself" mobilizations due to the changing forms and relations of production brought on by the soy complex. These are the new dynamics of agrarian change that we must continue to engage with and make known to the wider society. In combining access analysis, control grabbing and state theory within a framework of agrarian political economy inspired by the works of Byres (1996) and Bernstein (1996, 2010), I hope to contribute to our understanding of contemporary dynamics of agrarian change through the advancement of the politics of control and concepts such as productive exclusion, value-chain control, agrarian extractivism and the state-society-nexus, which, when applied to other sectors and places, may illuminate more generalizable trends and tendencies of agro-industrial capital's penetration into the countryside in the contemporary era.

Trajectories of Agrarian Change: Lessons and Implications

A number of broader implications can be drawn from this study for further scientific research, for policy making and for social movements. For researchers, several currents and directions of agrarian change point to important, yet understudied, areas for future research in agrarian studies. First, the amalgamation of agribusiness, pharmaceutical, chemical and petroleum companies such as the Monsanto-Bayer merger, or Shell-Cosan merger for sugarcane flex crop production (McKay et al. 2016), and the financialization of food and agriculture characterized by agro-commodity derivatives, farmland funds, agricultural risk managements and so on (Murphy, Burch and Clapp 2012; Fairbairn 2014; Isakson 2014; Ghosh 2010) require investigations in agrarian studies to go beyond the agricultural sector to broader analyses of sectoral linkages. This involves examining the relations between industrial and agricultural sectors. Second, the increasingly creative ways that capital has penetrated the countryside further require analyses that focus on access and control, rather than property and concessional rights.

Relatedly, this requires going beyond the rural to how and why people move between the urban and rural or have diversified livelihood strategies as farmers, rentiers, shopkeepers or rural and urban wage labourers. The functional dualism and resultant contradictory class positions of semiproletarians and petty bourgeois rentiers have significant implications for resistance and trajectories of agrarian change. Third, as extractive sectors become integrated at the corporate level, forms of resistance and organized mobilization must also integrate and form alliances. Revealing the extractive dynamics of agricultural production and reframing it as agrarian extractivism can challenge the legitimating discourse of industrial agriculture and potentially lead to strategic alliances among those struggling for social justice in (agro-)extractive sectors. More studies on agrarian extractivism across various agricultural sectors and case study sites will help develop and refine this concept. Fourth, the new relations between developing countries and emerging economies such as BRICS and some MICS require more in-depth critical analyses. China's investment, trade and financial relations with Bolivia, for example, have increased dramatically over the past ten years. In 2015, Chinese companies were awarded the majority of public contracts from the Bolivian state, while China's Export-Import Bank has become the country's largest financier. As bilateral trade increased eleven-fold from 2005 to 2016, China surpassed Brazil and the United States as Bolivia's primary source of imports. How the so-called Beijing Consensus differs from the Washington Consensus and its implications for agrarian change and resource control continue to unfold. Fifth, despite increased corporate control over the global food system, alternatives such as food sovereignty remain important, but they must be rigorously assessed for their viability and contradictions in the contemporary context. Many of the so-called neo-extractivist states in Latin America have poured significant funds into food sovereignty and food sovereignty–like programs, but do so with rents derived from resource extraction. Such profoundly contradictory models of development require further investigation into the limits and possibilities, convergences and contradictions of pursuing food sovereignty alternatives while remaining fiscally dependent on extractivist rents.

For researchers in Bolivia, this study points to the need to continue to investigate and reveal the challenges faced by smallholders during this transition in order to engage with, and put pressure on, state actors. If this trajectory of agrarian change continues, subsequent governments will face increased pressures as rural populations become surplus to the needs of capital accumulation and control over the countryside becomes further concentrated in the hands of a few. This could trigger widespread social discontent among various social movements, given the recent forms of contestation around TIPNIS, the Indigenous Fund, COMIBOL (Bolivia's state-owned mining company) and numerous other political scandals such as the former vice president's falsified academic credential and Morales's affair with a manager of China's CAMC Engineering Company. Morales's resignation has certainly left a power void, with various factions across the political spectrum vying to take state power. Alliances among social movements, scholar-activists and progressive state actors will be important to overcome conservative right-wing forces seeking a return to neoliberalism. Organic intellectuals in Bolivia such as those associated with the Comuna as well as critical NGOs and researchers associated with Fundación TIERRA, the Bolivian Documentation and Information Centre (Centro de Documentación e Información Bolivia), the Centre for Research and Promotion of Farmers (Centro de Investigación y Promoción del Campesinado), PROBIOMA and others need to continue to share their valuable research and open spaces for dialogue with state actors and social movements alike. For this study, people in Cuatro Cañadas and San Julián were very eager and happy to share their stories, experiences and challenges with me, in part because no one else was listening. One of the main purposes of this research was to provide an outlet for these stories to be shared and heard among a wider audience. Researchers need to continue to share these stories to uncover the reality faced by rural populations within the capitalist development of agriculture.

For policymakers and elected state managers, the findings of this study should be considered with a high sense of urgency and importance. The rural majority represented by smallholders have maintained, for the most part, formal rights to their land. This is extremely important for their livelihoods and the future of farming in the Bolivian lowlands. Before smallholders are forced to abandon these lands for reasons raised throughout this study, reformist state actors need to use their capacities and strategic positioning in order to effect change by engaging with allied forces in society. First of all, loopholes in the land ceiling need to be closed and applied retroactively so as to eliminate the continued existence of the latifundium and redistribute the land to the landless and smallholders. Second, there is a need to reorient rural and agricultural policies away from the agro-industrial and landlord bias by prioritizing the needs and interests of the rural majority of smallholders, including women and the youth. Bolivia's export-oriented agricultural development model has increased the country's dependence on food imports, making the country much more vulnerable to volatile commodity prices and food insecurity — far from any pathway towards food sovereignty. Third, the country needs to focus on industrializing and strengthening rural-urban, agriculture industry intersectoral linkages, which will generate employment opportunities through value-added processing and manufacturing. The so-called industrialization strategy to date has been one of importing value-added industrialized goods in order to extract resources for export. The soy complex has developed into a form of agrarian extractivism similar to the mining and hydrocarbon sectors. Fourth, the environmental and ecological crisis is real and imminent. The increased intensity and severity of the ENSO phenomenon caused major flooding and droughts in 2015–16. Farmers can no longer follow the regular planting and harvesting cycles. Yields are extremely volatile as soil fertility is in decline and new pests appear every year and are widespread. Deforestation is not only exacerbating these environmental crises but threatening Indigenous livelihoods. Stronger environmental policies are needed and cannot be detached from the model of agricultural development being pursued.

For social movements and their NGO allies and scholar-activists, this study points to the importance of forming broader alliances and converging social movement struggles against a common enemy or set of policies. This is, in part, the purpose of reframing certain types of capitalist industrial agriculture as agrarian extractivism — to facilitate the convergence of those working in and around (agro-)extractive sectors. Furthermore, historically, it has been the convergence of social movements that has managed to shift the balance of forces in society and open the way for transformative political and social change. This was demonstrated in the revolutionary struggles in the 1950s and once again fifty years later, during the struggles against neoliberal policies that eventually brought Morales and MAS to state power. The political legitimacy of MAS, as a self-proclaimed "government of social movements," has hinged upon its relationship with the principal social movements represented by the Pacto de Unidad. Despite the fracturing of the Pacto de Unidad in recent years, its social bases remain vibrant and strong with common struggles largely based on various forms of exclusion and threats to their livelihoods brought on by *extractivismo*. History shows that it is in the best interest of these movements to continue to form loose alliances to increase their strength and influence in numbers, representing peasants, Indigenous people, women and trade unions among the rural and urban working classes. While their relations with the state are important, their autonomy is crucial if they are to maintain their ability to criticize and hold state actors accountable. Furthermore, the politics within the movements are equally as important so as to ensure that individual political clientelism and *caciques* do not emerge that use their position within the movement for self-gain. I hope this study provides some perspective on these issues and particularly on the specific class positions of smallholders in the soy complex today.

Epilogue

The rise of MAS and presidential election of Evo Morales represented a new era in Bolivian history and politics, as the country's first Indigenous president vowed to rollback neoliberal policies and pursue a pro-poor socially just and inclusive development agenda. Resource nationalism, a redistribution of wealth, agrarian reform and anti-imperialist discourses rejecting the neoliberal model of development were applauded and supported by the majority. Discourses of food sovereignty, rights to Mother Nature and *vivir bien* replaced capitalist discourses about the need for economic growth and pursuit of an age of high mass consumption. The so-called government of social movements transformed state-society relations as the country's most prominent social movements became incorporated into the state. Indigenous people, peasants, miners, trade union workers and women became empowered, symbolically, politically and materially. Political participation was an important factor in this process, and key social movements were invited to draft a new Constitution and movement leaders were appointed to ministry-level positions. Morales's history, identity and discourse enhanced the state's degree of legitimacy — the country's majority could finally identify with their leader. But as movement leaders transitioned to state managers, they became gradually absorbed and partially coopted by the state apparatus. Many social movements lost much of their autonomy to challenge and criticize the MAS government for fear that they would lose state support and access to resources and be labelled as the opposition and against the "process of change."

The commodities boom increased the fiscal capacity of the state, and extractivist rents have been distributed to the poor through cash transfers and state-led projects. What has transpired, however, is a high degree of political clientelism, as state revenues are transferred to regions and their movements' leaders in exchange for political support. Morales explicitly warned the general public that if they did not vote for the MAS representative in municipal or departmental election, they would not receive support from the state.[1] As commodity prices and extractive-based revenues have fallen, MAS has increased extractivist expansion into frontiers — for lithium, natural gas, minerals and agro-commodities. Extractivist rents and the increased accumulation of capital were necessary for MAS's political legitimacy. Yet, these dual functions of the capitalist state are contradictory, as the state's model of *extractivismo* has failed to transform the unequal socioeconomic structures of production, distribution, consumption and accumulation and maintained an economy based on primary product exports controlled by market oligopolies. But while the state's legitimacy has been compromised due to its extractive overreach in the hydrocarbon and mining sectors (Pueblo 2016), including the infamous TIPNIS conflict (Webber 2015), this has not been the case in terms of the development and expansion of the soy complex as a type of agrarian extractivism.

This study has provided a critical analysis, grounded in agrarian political economy, into how and to what extent the development and expansion of the agro-industrial soy complex is transforming agrarian social relations in Bolivia's eastern lowlands and the changing state-society-relations associated with these processes. Forms of exclusion, mechanisms of control and value appropriation and the extractive dynamics of the soy complex have been revealed. The politics of control has helped us understand the role and nature of the state and the relations between classes in society. This critique is written with a sense of urgency, as these processes of agrarian change continue to unfold and threaten the rural majority. Despite the unpromising trajectories alluded to throughout this study, such directions of change in no way represent predetermined outcomes. Actors from both the state and society are able to effect change and pursue a pathway away from *extractivismo* and towards food sovereignty and *vivir bien*. It is my hope that this study contributes to efforts towards that change.

NOTE

1. In a national television broadcast on Gigavision, Morales stated the following: "I just want to tell our grandparents and future generations: how can I work with the city of El Alto with people from the 'right'? I'm not going to work [with these people], brothers. If you want more work there is [MAS candidate] Edgar Patana, if they want more work there is [MAS candidate] Felipa Huanca. Make a reflection, depends on you" (Mealla 2015; author's translation).

REFERENCES

Akram-Lodhi, A. Haroon, and Cristóbal Kay. 2009. *Peasants and Globalization: Political Economy, Rural Transformation and the Agrarian Question*. A. Haroon Akram-lodhi and Cristóbal Kay (eds.). Routledge ISS Studies in Rural Livelihoods. London and New York: Routledge.

Bernstein, Henry. 1996. "Agrarian Questions Then and Now." *Journal of Peasant*

Studies, 24, 1–2: 22–59.

____. 2010. *Class Dynamics of Agrarian Change*. Halifax and Winnipeg: Fernwood Publishing.

Borras, Saturnino M. Jr., Jennifer C. Franco, Sergio Gomez, Cristóbal Kay, and Max Spoor. 2012. "Land Grabbing in Latin America and the Caribbean." *Journal of Peasant Studies*, 39, 3–4): 845–872.

Byres, Terence J. 1996. *Capitalism from Above and Capitalism from Below: An Essay in Comparative Political Economy*. UK: Palgrave Macmillan.

Fairbairn, Madeleine. 2014. "'Like Gold with Yield': Evolving Intersections between Farmland and Finance." *Journal of Peasant Studies*, 41, 5: 1–19.

Ghosh, Jayati. 2010. "The Unnatural Coupling: Food and Global Finance." *Journal of Agrarian Change*, 10, 1: 72–86.

Goodman, David, Bernardo Sorj, and John Wilkinson. 1987. *From Farming to Biotechnology: A Theory of Agro-Industrial Development*. Oxford, UK: Basil Blackwell.

Isakson, S. Ryan. 2014. "Food and Finance: The Financial Transformation of Agro-Food Supply Chains." *Journal of Peasant Studies*, 41, 5: 749–775.

McKay, Ben, Sérgio Sauer, Ben Richardson, and Roman Herre. 2016. "The Political Economy of Sugarcane Flexing: Initial Insights from Brazil, Southern Africa and Cambodia." *Journal of Peasant Studies*, 43, 1: 195–223.

Mealla, Luis. 2015. "Si la Derecha Gana en La Paz y El Alto, Evo No Trabajará con Ella." <la-razon.com/nacional/animal_electoral/derecha-Paz-Alto-Evo-trabajara_0_2227577305.html>

Murphy, Sophia, David Burch, and Jennifer Clapp. 2012. *Cereal Secrets: The World's Largest Commodity Traders and Global Trends in Agriculture*. Oxfam Research Report.

Pueblo, Defensor del. 2016. *Sin Los Pueblos Indígenas No Hay Estado Plurinacional*. La Paz.

Ribot, Jesse C., and Nancy Lee Peluso. 2003. "A Theory of Access." *Rural Sociology* 68, 2: 153–181.

Soto Baquero, Fernando, and Sergio Gómez. 2012. *Dinámicas Del Mercado de La Tierra En América Latina y El Caribe: Concentracíon y Extranjerización*. Food and Agriculture Organization of the United Nations (FAO). Rome: FAO.

Webber, Jeffrey R. 2015. "Revolution against 'Progress': Neo-Extractivism, the Compensatory State, and the Tipnis Conflict in Bolivia." In Susan J. Spronk and Jeffrey R. Webber (eds.), *Crisis and Contradiction: Marxist Perspectives on Latin America in the Global Political Economy*. Leiden: Brill.

Weis, Tony. 2010. "The Accelerating Biophysical Contradictions of Industrial Capitalist Agriculture." *Journal of Agrarian Change*, 10, 3: 315–341.

World Bank. 2007. *World Development Report 2008: Agriculture for Development. World Development Report 2008*. Washington.

Index

Acknowledgments

In 2014–15, I moved to a small community in the heart of rural Bolivia's soybean zone to undertake the research which ultimately resulted in this book. I am extremely grateful to the people of Cuatro Cañadas and neighbouring San Julián for welcoming me with open arms; for their hospitality; and for taking the time to share their stories, histories and everyday experiences of life on the land. In particular, I want to thank Betty Rueda and Benigno Duran, Andrés Chuviru, Paulino Sánchez, Abrahm Fehr, Ronal Escalera, Lisandra Fernandez Cutiño and Waldemar Rojas — your help, support and friendship made this research possible.

Carrying out this type of fieldwork in Bolivia would never have been possible without the support from Fundación TIERRA. A special thanks to the entire TIERRA team, and especially to Gonzalo Colque for facilitating the institutional support and for the continued collaboration and friendship.

I owe special thanks to Jun Borras, Max Spoor, Murat Arsel, Henry Veltmeyer and Annette Desmarais, who provided critical comments and helpful suggestions on earlier drafts and for which this book greatly benefitted. Any remaining errors are, of course, my own.

Writing a book is an arduous process. I want to thank my friends and colleagues at the International Institute of Social Studies and in the BRICS Initiative for Critical Agrarian Studies network for their support and for inspiring me to develop many of the ideas that appear in this book. To Carolina, thank you for your patience, support and guidance throughout this entire process.

Many thanks to the Series Editors — Henry Veltmeyer, Annette Desmarais and Raúl Delgado Wise — for the invitation to contribute to this exciting book series on Critical Development Studies. Thanks to the Social Sciences and Humanities Research Council of Canada for providing financial support to carry out this research. Finally, many thanks to the folks at Fernwood — especially Errol Sharpe, Beverley Rach, Deb Mathers, Brenda Conroy and Erin Seatter — for their excellent work carrying out the many tasks involved in the editorial and production process.

www.ingramcontent.com/pod-product-compliance
Ingram Content Group UK Ltd.
Pitfield, Milton Keynes, MK11 3LW, UK
UKHW021833100926
8556IPUK00004B/319

9 781788 531382